THE
MACMILLAN
BOOK
OF ORNAMENTAL GARDENING

OTTO HAHN

THE MACMILLAN BOOK

OF ORNAMENTAL GARDENING

Translated by Susan H. Ray

COLLIER BOOKS
MACMILLAN PUBLISHING COMPANY
New York

COLLIER MACMILLAN PUBLISHERS
London

Macmillan Publishing Company
866 Third Avenue, New York, N.Y. 10022
Collier Macmillan Canada, Inc.

Title of the original German edition:
ZIERGEHÖLZE
© 1981 BLV Verlagsgesellschaft mbH, München

English translation copyright © 1985 by Macmillan Publishing Company, a division of Macmillan, Inc.

Library of Congress Cataloging in Publication Data

Hahn, Otto.
    The Macmillan book of ornamental gardening.

    Translation of: Ziergehölze.
    1. Ornamental trees.   2. Ornamental shrubs.
I. Title.
SB435.H2613   1985   635.9′77   85-7275
ISBN 0-02-063130-8

10 9 8 7 6 5 4 3 2 1

Printed in Germany

Introduction

Planning

Home gardeners frequently purchase trees and shrubs spontaneously, and then neglect to plant them in the location best suited to their optimal development. Therefore, before the purchase of any plants, you should make it a general rule to carefully design the new arrangement of an already existing garden or the landscaping of a totally new one. This is particularly important in the case of ornamentals because, in comparison with annuals or bushes, these trees and shrubs can be expected to have a long life span. And as we all know, once a tree or shrub has begun to flourish, even if in the wrong spot, we are more likely to let it stay where it is than to take the trouble to transplant it! This happens, typically, to plants that have been placed too close to the property line or too close to the house.

The most important decision in the planning stage concerns the type of garden you want, whether it should be an atrium garden, have a country or perhaps field flower emphasis, or feature a pond or stream. There are other variables, however, that also have to be taken into consideration, and these include the environment; the size and topography of the planned garden; its location; light, soil, and water conditions; and the eventual amount of care the garden will require.

Environment: The type and size of a garden are influenced by its immediate and wider environment, and the gardener is well advised to consider these factors and their specific characteristics when planning a garden. The garden that is meant to enhance a modern house, for instance, should be appropriate to its surroundings and not have a rustic, country look. Consideration should also be given to the shade cast by other buildings or trees when selecting new plants.

Size: The size of the garden plot plays an important role in the selection as well as the later development of woody plants. The ultimate dimensions of these plants are frequently underestimated, and this can cause an initial poor choice of location with not enough surrounding space. Specific references regarding the space needs of the various plants have been incorporated in the individual descriptions that make up the body of this guide. The spaces between the larger specimens that seem rather bare during the growing stages can be filled in with plants that remain small or with bushes that gradually can be removed as the ornamental trees or shrubs attain their mature size.

Topography: Because of today's high prices, the land available for a garden is usually relatively small. However, if the opportunity to purchase a larger site should present itself, preference should be given to a rolling landscape, for this type of topography displays ornamentals at their best and increases the ways in which they can be used.

Location: Where the garden is situated also helps determine the choice of plants. Particular attention should be given to elevation and exposure, factors that can have a considerable effect on the garden's climatic conditions. A piece of property near a sizable lake in a somewhat lower altitude will enjoy a particularly even climate, whereas a site in the foothills will be characterized by a more rugged climate and thus preclude use of most of the sensitive plants.

Light: Light conditions are affected by buildings, trees, and exposures. The choice of plants is directly dependent upon the amount of full sun that shines on the plot.

Soil: Woody plants have definite and differing requirements of the type of soil they need. Many leafy plants and conifers prefer a soil that is medium heavy to heavy, sufficiently moist and rich in nutrients, while rhododendrons and azaleas need a moist, acidic soil containing humus. Because of the variation in requirements, you must expect a certain restriction in your choice of ornamentals. This problem is frequently remedied, however, by improving the soil with additives or fertilizers.

Water Conditions: Disregarding periods of drought and those geographic areas that do not normally receive much precipitation, the natural amount of rainfall prevalent in our latitude is usually sufficient to meet the needs of good-sized shrubs and trees. As far as the optimal amount of moisture is concerned, it is always a good idea to set up a conveniently situated outside faucet.

Eventual Care: In planning a garden and its layout, sufficient attention is seldom given to the type and amount of care necessary to keep it up. The amount of care and time required to maintain an extensive and imaginative arrangement of bushes and summer flowers can soon become overwhelming. The proper selection of plants under careful consideration of existing conditions can contribute tremendously to the easing, if not the saving, of a lot of work.

Soil Preparation and Requirements

The fact that woody plants as a group make varying requirements as far as the type of soil is concerned has already been mentioned. Specific information concerning these factors is an essential part of the individual descriptions that follow. Since marshy or moorland plants like azaleas and heaths can only thrive in an acidic soil rich in humus, these needs will have to be met. Equally obvious is the fact that extreme soils, such as sandy or clay soils, in their original state are not suitable for very many plants. Nevertheless, both extremes can be improved by mixing in appropriate additives so that they will support a great variety of plants.

The following basics about soil should be kept in mind: humus in the form of compost, peat, or fertilizer always has a compensatory or equalizing effect, which means that after adding humus, sandy soil will retain more water, and heavy clay or loamy soil will become looser. The duration of the desired effect depends upon the stability of the humus; fertilizing peat, for instance, has a longer effect than compost. Moreover, the lighter the soil, the quicker the decomposition of the humus material. This is why mixing additional sand and commercially produced non-porous flakes into heavy soils, is sometimes recommended, whereas for lighter soils the addition of porous and spongy material is appropriate.

In the case of so-called virgin or untreated soils, which are, unfortunately, frequently found in new development sites, manuring with a green fertilizer before the planting of trees or shrubs is advisable. If the soil is heavy, one can use rape-seed or various types of legumens for this purpose; for lighter soils *Phacelias* or various legumens can be added. This initial treatment with a green fertilizer vitalizes the virgin soil and simultaneously adds humus, which, in turn, ensures a further improvement. The best time to do the green manuring is in the fall so that the fertilizer has a chance to decompose by spring when the trees and shrubs should be planted. The actual scheduling depends upon the type of manure used as well as upon its rate of decomposition. Further details can be obtained from a professional garden and seed shop.

Choosing and Purchasing Plants

In addition to choosing ornamental trees and shrubs suitable to their location, the quality of the individual specimen plays an important role as far as its later growth is concerned. It is understandable that an inexperienced gardener will have difficulties in judging the quality of a plant, especially if the deciduous ones have already lost their leaves. In the final analysis, however, the purchaser is most interested in how the plant will look in his or her garden. Thus it is advisable to familiarize oneself with the information contained in the relevant literature on the subject and in nursery catalogues. As far as how the plant looks is concerned, the ideal procedure is to visit a nursery at the peak of the blooming season and to choose each ornamental plant from the wide selection that well-known nurseries and municipal and botanical gardens make available for just this viewing purpose. This is particularly important for deciduous plants, for they are generally sold in a leafless state. Exceptions to this are the so-called container plants, which come in plastic containers and can be bought and planted at any time of the year.

In order to take advantage of the largest possible selection of attractive plants, you should plan to purchase ornamental trees and shrubs well before the end of their selling season. As a general rule, you can assume that nurseries and garden centers trade only in healthy and unblemished specimens. There are several organizations and associations in the United States that provide a regulatory function as far as quality, quarantine, and fair and accurate advertising are concerned. These include, among others, the U.S. Department of Agriculture, the Mail Order Association of Nurserymen, and the

American Association of Nurserymen. Each of them publishes relevant guidelines and specifications for the trade. One can assume that most nurseries and garden centers abide by these guidelines and specifications, but this does not mean that the purchaser should ignore some very critical factors:

Time of Purchase: With the exception of container plants, which can be bought and planted at any time of the year, most trees and shrubs should be planted during the period between October and March or April. If the climatic conditions are favorable, it is best to plant in the fall so that the ornamentals will have time to develop some roots during the milder portions of the winter and can thus set their shoots more quickly and bloom more profusely the following spring. In areas of more rugged climate, it is advisable to wait until after the end of winter before planting, because only then will the danger of frost or drought be reduced. In locations with heavier soils practically no roots at all are developed under severe winter weather conditions. Thus, there is nothing to mitigate the ravages of these natural phenomena.

When transplanting container plants during the warm summer months, an ample supply of water should be provided. The lack of adequate moisture can result in damage that is frequently irreversible or takes a very long time to be remedied.

Deciduous Plants: These are available in various forms, as large and small trees, and as bushes, shrubs, or small plants. Shrubs are frequently purchased for smaller gardens, and each should have at least three, if not more, healthy branches showing a strong growth pattern. Moderately to vigorously growing shrubs like *Forsythia* or *Philadelphus* should have branches about 3' long. These should be stiff but somewhat elastic and their bark should be free of shrivels and wrinkles, which indicate drought damage. Spring bloomers, such as lilacs or azaleas, should have clearly formed, tight, plump buds. Shrubs that do not bloom in the spring are frequently cut back in the nursery at the time of purchase; this is also true for plants with excessively long roots.

Evergreen Woody Plants and Conifers: This group is usually sold in the form of container plants or with a covered root ball. Such "balled" plants have jute or some other protective material wrapped around the root ball. When buying evergreen leafy plants such as holly or conifers, for instance, one should look for a well-shaped, species-specific appearance with healthy lateral branches and healthy leaves or needles. Spotted leaves or needles as well as signs of nibbling indicate disease or insect damage. Bald spots on conifers usually stay that way and do not turn green with time. The only way they can be covered up is by the growth of the plant in later years. In the case of small, less vigorously growing conifers, it is best not to count on this growth to disguise imperfections. Tall, narrow, cone-shaped conifers should not have any holes or open spaces in their foliage.

Woody Clinging Vines: This group of plants is usually available for purchase during the hibernation period, although as a result of increasing use of larger containers, many nurseries and garden centers are beginning to feature them year-round. The advantage of buying them during the hibernation period is that one usually gets a better idea of the actual size of the plant.

Botanical Nomenclature

Botanists and horticulturists are frequently reproached by lay gardeners for using complicated, botanical names for plants instead of their common English designations. This is understandable when one contemplates such tongue-twisters as *Chaemaecyparis nootkatensis* or *Cotinus coggygria.* In many cases, however, there is no problem at all, for most of the popular plants are also known by their familiar common names.

International guidelines that are occasionally subjected to revisions concerning their accuracy form the basis of the botanical and horticultural system of nomenclature. This system greatly facilitates the not inconsiderable international exchange and sale of plants, and it has also had a positive effect on and favorable reception in the whole field, especially at gatherings such as congresses and conventions. The common names that have developed in the individual countries over the years are frequently imaginative and descriptive, but this descriptiveness cannot guarantee clear communication given the enormous number of plants under consideration at any one time. It frequently happens that there is more than one name for one and the same plant, and this is true for almost any language. *Forsythia,* for instance, is known by many names, and it is not uncommon that some species are mistaken for others. Since the scientific and horticultural communities appreciate the difficulties the hobbyist encounters with these botanical names, attempts have been made to alleviate such problems by publishing handbooks and guides which give both designations, the scientific as well as the common. Of course, the home gardener is not expected to walk around with such a reference work tucked under his or her arm, but a rudimentary knowledge of botanical nomenclature does come in handy when buying plants. Moreover, the purchaser can take it for granted that catalogues and advertisements from respected nurseries and garden or seed centers are designed according to this system. This is also true for the more serious literature and journals in the gardening field. To make it easier for the reader, the following descriptions of ornamental trees and shrubs are arranged according to their botanical designations, and these are followed, wherever possible, by their common English names.

Since the scientific names of some plants have been changed as a result of the constant examination of these designations for accuracy, and since these changes can very easily lead to confusion, the previous, and now revised, names are given as synonyms in the text.

THE STRUCTURE OF BOTANICAL NAMES: The composition of the botanical designations of individual plants follows a uniform pattern. Each plant has at least two names: the first name, which is capitalized, refers to the genus, *Abies,* for example. The second name, with a small initial letter, refers to the species, as for example, *nordmanniana.* The full botanical name is therefore *Abies nordmanniana,* or, in its abbreviated form, *A. nordmanniana.* The common English name is the *Nordmann Fir.*

Origin of Botanical Names: The traditional names of plants are often very old. This explains why many generic names reflect the latinized form of the common name, since science uses classical languages like Latin or Greek. The reason behind a certain name can be the origin of the plant, as, for example, *Castanea,* the edible chestnut tree that is indigenous to Castana in Thessaly. Sometimes recognition of a researcher can be the force behind the generic name. This is the case with *Robinia,* which was named in honor of the horticulturist Robin, who introduced the plant to Europe around 1600.

The species name, too, can sometimes be traced back to a person. Many times, though, the species designation expresses definite characteristics, as for example, *alba* (white), *rubra* (red), *gracilis* (ornamental, graceful). Even a comparison with other plants can lead to a species name: *salicifolia* (with leaves like a willow) or *ilicifolia* (with leaves like a holly plant).

The species name is frequently followed by a variety name. The variety designation thus represents additional information beyond genus and species, perhaps an additional subdivision. Examples of this are *Buddleia davidii* "Royal Red" and *Buddleia davidii* "Empire Blue," which differ from each other only in the color of their blossoms. If a specific variety of a specific genus and species is desired, all three names will be needed when you purchase the plant. Thus, you should not ask for red *polyantha* roses, but a very specific variety of these roses, such as "Swiss Greeting." If you keep these few guidelines in mind, you should have no trouble in finding the exact plant you want.

Planting

After you have chosen the desired specimens, the actual planting can begin. There are some definite steps to this procedure, however, and they should be heeded. First of all, it is a good idea to line the plants up before actually digging them in; if they, and particularly the roots, look a bit wilted, they should be soaked in water for a few hours. This is impossible, of course, in the case of balled plants like conifers, but it can certainly be done with azaleas and rhododendrons. If they look fresh and sprightly and ready to be planted, all they will need is a brief sprinkling of the above-ground parts as well as of the roots, followed by a temporary covering with moist sack-cloth or tin foil. Since the roots of roses are usually cut back at the time of purchase, rose bushes should always be placed in water overnight so that the tissues can be completely drenched.

The next important step after protecting the plants against drying out (and perhaps even thoroughly watering them) is the digging of the holes. Regardless of whether you are working in an already existing garden that is going to be completely rearranged or in a brand-new one, the whole area to be planted should be dug up and the soil prepared and improved. Only then are you ready to dig the holes, and these should be somewhat larger than the root balls or the circumference of the root system. If the roots have been cut back to any degree, be sure to place the plants with the cut edge extending

downward. If only a few plants are to be added to an already existing garden, the holes should be as large and as deep as possible so there will be enough room around the roots to add humus. If the soil is packed solid or if the plants can be expected to grow larger, you should loosen up the soil around and under the hole. It never hurts to add a little moist humus-containing material in conditions like these. The easiest way to do it is to mix moist peat into the soil that has been dug up as well as into the loosened soil surrounding the hole. It would be a mistake to use fresh barnyard manure here, because this type of fertilizer burns the roots.

The roots of woody plants, and especially those bound in root balls, should be distributed as evenly as possible in the hole. Once this is done, the hole can be filled. This final step is best done with the help of another person, for while one fills the hole, the other can hold the plant straight and carefully jiggle it around to make sure that no empty cavities are left between the roots. Once the hole has been filled, the loose earth around the plant should be carefully packed down so that the roots can take hold in their new location. Most woody plants, with the exception of roses and a few others, should be placed just as deeply in their new location as in their original one. The transition zone between the above- and below-ground parts of the plant is the root stem, which is generally a different color than either the trunk or the shoots and is usually smeared with dirt. This root stem should be buried in the ground.

A gentle stamping down of the soil around the newly planted shrub or tree results in the formation of a slight gully surrounding the plant. This, in turn, prevents water from draining off to the side and thus away from the roots. The plant should be amply watered, and the moisture should ooze as deeply as possible into the root system, for this is absolutely necessary for the growth of woody plants. They should also be watered at regular intervals during any prolonged dry spell. A rapid evaporation of water can be prevented by covering the newly planted spot with compost, moist peat, spoiled hay, or leaves. Such a covering frequently attracts mice, but there are ways of dealing with this problem.

The same procedure should be followed in the case of balled or container plants. The covering around the root ball should be removed only after the plant has been positioned in the hole. If plastic containers cannot be safely removed from the roots without doing damage, they should be cut away, but again, only after the plant is already in the hole.

At this stage in the planting process, many woody plants will require some pruning. This may already have been done in the nursery or garden center at the time of purchase. If it hasn't, you should do so yourself, for a careful pruning is the basis for the further growth and development of the plant's "skeleton." The weaker shoots and branches should be completely removed and the more vigorous ones cut back by a third to a half. In some cases, frost or drought damage will determine the extent of the pruning. If the damage is extensive, an additional cutting back to the healthy wood may be necessary the following spring. Whenever possible, try to cut back to where the terminal bud faces outward. This has a positive effect on the eventual shape of the plant, for if this bud faces inward, the branch will either be too steep or else it, too, will grow in toward the center of the plant.

Additional Tips

Most ornamental woody plants need a lot more than just proper planting, including the following tasks that can contribute greatly to the overall flourishing of the plant as well as to your enjoyment of a beautiful garden.

Care of the Soil: During the first few years after planting, the soil surrounding the ornamental tree or shrub should be kept open, which means free of weeds. The urgency and duration of this weeding is directly dependent upon the growth habits of the plant: if it has a less vigorous growth, it should be kept carefully weeded for a longer time. Insufficient or improper weeding can lead to a noticeable stunting. As soon as the ornamental plant reaches its mature height and width, this extensive weeding can be reduced. A good way to avoid a great deal of this work is to introduce ornamental ground covers or hardy annuals which tend to suppress the growth of weeds. As long as the ground is kept open, weeds can be controlled by mulching (or covering) with compost, moist peat, spoiled hay, etc. Special weed killers (herbicides) may also be used, but this is neither necessary nor recommended in home gardens. A good rule of thumb is: the fewer chemicals the better.

Fertilizing: A distinction should be made here between organic fertilizing with barnyard manure, compost, peat, and so forth, and the addition of mineral manures known as commercial fertilizers. These fertilizers contain ''commercially'' produced mineral additives (such as nitrate of soda), or are processed in factories using natural raw materials (potash and phosphorus, for example). However, regardless of their source it has been scientifically demonstrated that as far as chemicals are concerned plants take their nourishment in the same form from both organic fertilizers and commercially produced inorganic ones.

The organic manures contain very little nourishment in comparison with commercial mineral fertilizers. Those richest in nutrients are barnyard manure and compost, and the poorest, as far as nutrients are concerned, is the peat moss most frequently used in home gardens. The primary effect of organic fertilizers can be obtained through the addition of humus. However, since ornamental woody plants frequently need a quantity of nutrients not usually provided by organic fertilizers, most horticulturists recommend using a variety of organic and inorganic fertilizers, usually as a combination of peat and mineral additives. The commercially produced ''complete fertilizers'' are recommended for this purpose, for they contain the basic nutrients nitrogen, phosphorus, and potash. Further details about the composition and application of these fertilizers can be obtained either from a professional horticulturist or from the package. For those woody plants that need lime, fertilizing should be supplemented every few years with carbonate of lime.

Proponents of purely organic manures can obtain from professional sources various substitute products consisting of blood and bone meal, horn shavings, and dried bird dung (guano). These manures are highly recommended for their positive results, but their odor can sometimes be unpleasant.

Protection: Providing plants with some sort of chemical protection is frequently overdone in small and home gardens, and this is particularly true when it comes to ornamentals. If the tips of young shoots fall victim to a slight infestation of leaf-lice or aphids, the removal of the affected tips is often sufficient; there is no need to spray immediately with highly toxic insecticides. Preventive measures such as proper location, proper choice of species and variety, and optimal care are more important than the premature use of chemicals. You should resort to these means only after a certain tolerance threshhold has been exceeded. If insecticides are needed, they should be chosen whenever possible from among those with an organic base. And, of course, the insecticide that is least toxic for man and animals should be selected.

Pruning: Frequent pruning is unnecessary for many woody plants. Those that bloom from July onward are the ones that usually need the most cutting back. Their buds are set in the spring of the current year. The ornamentals that bloom in spring have already set their buds in the previous year. This is why you have to be much more conservative when giving these plants their winter pruning, for cutting them back can decimate the extent of the bloom. Apart from a necessary trim from time to time to encourage new growth, routine pruning measures should be restricted to a trimming of the shape during or after the bloom. Fruit-bearing ornamentals such as the crab apples should not be cut beyond an occasional "rejuvenation." Shrubs like the Japanese Maple, which are planted because of their ornamental foliage, generally do not need cutting back. At the most, an occasional removal of individual branches might be undertaken to improve the shape. Whether you prune a lot or only a little, the following guidelines ought to be heeded: always use sharp instruments; don't leave any branch or shoot stumps (this promotes the growth of fungus); and always paint the cut surface with special preparations to promote healing.

Trimming: When older shrubs grow too tall and begin to lose their foliage from the bottom up, they should be trimmed. This means cutting away the old branches in favor of the younger, new ones. After removal of the old shoots, many woody shrubs develop adventive buds where the branch was cut. Old, overhanging branches are then set off against the younger, more vigorous shoots. This emphasis on the newer growth is recommended at intervals of several years, especially in the case of spring bloomers like *Forsythia*. Those plants that bloom from July onward can be cut back to the ground, if need be. This applies, for example, to the *Buddleia* family, but all that this group usually needs is the routine removal of individual aged branches.

Trimming of Hedges: Many mistakes are made in the trimming of hedges. This is usually due to the desire to have a hedge as dense and tall as possible in the shortest possible time. This goal can only be realized, however, with relatively large and densely growing hedge plants. If you start out with smaller varieties, it can take years before the hedge reaches its desired height and density. An initial more vigorous growth can be attained by neglecting the annual cutting back of the tips and lateral branches, but this will ultimately not lead to the desired density and vigorous growth of the hedge because, by not cutting back, the growth will soon lack the necessary stimulation. If the hedge is meant to remain dense, it needs an annual cutting back. When doing this, you should be careful to keep the lower portions of the hedge wider than the upper parts. If this is not done, the hedge will suffer from a lack of light on its lower parts and will gradually lose its lower foliage and take on that "leggy" look.

Key to the Symbols

Height: height in inches or feet
Diameter: diameter in inches or feet
Soil: recommended type of soil

1   ordinary, fertilized garden soil, no particular requirements

2   porous, light soil

3   heavy, compactible soil

4   humus-containing, slightly acidic soil

5   calcareous soil, high lime content

IV–VII: blooming season (here, for example, April to July)

*   ornamental fruit
E   evergreen
!!!   poisonous

Explanation of Color Code

Blue: evergreen woody plant
Green: deciduous woody plant
Pink: ornamental blossoms or fruit

Illustrations

When there are three or four illustrations to a page, the consecutive descriptions refer to the illustrations in the following order: upper left, upper right, lower left, lower right.

If there is no particular reference in the text, the illustration is that of the described species or variety.

Pages 16–109 describe blooming leafy or needle plants, whereas pages 110–125 concentrate on creeping and climbing vines.

Abies nordmanniana   Nordmann Fir

Height: 50'–80'   Diameter: 13'–20'   Soil: 1   ❊   E

Origin: Caucasus. **Characteristics:** If they are surrounded by sufficient open space *A. nordmanniana* grows into tall, straight trees with sweeping horizontal branches. They are covered with lateral branches right down to the ground. For this reason, *A. nordmanniana* is a very ornamental conifer. **Growing Conditions:** The Nordmann Fir flourishes well in central European conditions and needs ordinary soil with an abundant supply of water but no standing water. **Recommendations:** *A. nordmanniana* is well suited as a solitary specimen or as part of a group of trees in large gardens or parks.

Abies koreana   Korean Fir

Height: 50'   Diameter: 6½'–10'   Soil: 1   ❊   E

Origin: Korea. **Characteristics:** The bristlelike, upright needles have a highly ornamental effect. The indicated height of 50' is not always attained, partly because this fir does not form an apical shoot. The Alpine variety is rarely taller than 6½'. The cones (illustration lower left) stand upright and have a purplish-violet color. **Growing Conditions:** Ordinary garden soil is advantageous for the growth of this tree. It should be planted in a somewhat protected location during its early years. **Recommendations:** Because of its low growth and the availability of the Alpine dwarf varieties, the Korean Fir is appropriate for smaller gardens of varying types.

Abies procera   Noble Fir

Height: 65'   Diameter: 16'   Soil: 1   ❊   E

Origin: Western North America. **Characteristics:** This fir tree, previously known as *A. nobilis,* has a dense and unparted needle growth on its younger shoots. The bluish-green needles can grow to a length of 1½". They tend to curve upward to a certain extent. The lower third of each branch is thickly covered with needles. A point of interest is that *A. procera* is considered especially pest-resistant. **Varieties and Species:** The variety "Glauca" (illustration lower right) is more frequently cultivated than the species *A. procera;* it has bluish-green needles and is very hardy. *A. concolor* is a very popular fir tree indigenous to the United States. It has a pointed pyramidal shape with horizontal branches and attains a height of up to 80'. Its needles are gray-green, sometimes appearing bluish. It needs a normal central European climate and ordinary soil conditions with an ample supply of water. Distributed varieties include "Candicans" with whitish blue-green needles and "Violacea," whose needles have a violet tinge. **Recommendations:** *A. procera* blends well in large gardens and parks. Moreover, this species of Noble Fir, especially the variety "Glauca," can be used for ornamental purposes.

16

Acer ginnala   Amur Maple

Origin: China, Japan, and Manchuria. **Characteristics:** Large bush or fairly small tree with greenish-yellow blossoms, shiny red fruits, and autumn coloration ranging from yellow to purple (illustration upper left). **Growing Conditions:** Rather tolerant with regard to climate and soil. **Recommendations:** Well suited as a solitary specimen for smaller to medium-sized gardens, but it can also be planted in groups in large parks.

Acer japonicum   Fullmoon Maple

Origin: Japan. **Characteristics:** Treelike bush with a broadly domed top. The leaves are lobed, with glorious autumn colors. **Growing Conditions:** *A. japonicum* is rather sensitive and therefore prefers protected spots. The soil should be quite moist but well drained. **Varieties:** "Aconitifolium" with leaves that resemble those of the Aconitum family and are reddish in color. "Aureum" (illustration upper right) has yellow leaves. **Recommendations:** Well suited for smaller to medium-sized gardens as a solitary specimen.

Acer negundo   Ash Maple, Box Elder

Origin: North America. **Characteristics:** Large bush or tree with ornamental leaves. The blossoms appear in May in the form of attractive overhanging clusters. **Growing Conditions:** Likes a sunny spot and a sufficiently moist soil rich in nutrients with no standing water. **Varieties:** "Auratum" with yellow leaves and reddish stalks. "Variegatum" (illustration lower left) with green and white variegated leaves. **Recommendations:** Can be displayed to advantage in larger gardens and smaller parks. The Box Elder stands out well against a predominantly green background.

Acer palmatum   Japanese Maple

Origin: Japan. **Characteristics:** Ornamental shrub or small tree with a broad and rounded crown and ornamental blossoms and leaves. **Growing Conditions:** *A. palmatum* needs a protected location with a porous, slightly acidic humus soil. Improvement is possible by adding moist peat. **Varieties:** "Atropurpureum" with purplish-red blossoms and leaves; smaller in size than the parent species. "Dissectum" (see lower right) with deeply dissected leaves that turn yellow in the fall. **Recommendations:** Best suited as a solitary specimen.

Aesculus hippocastanum   Horse Chestnut

Height: 80′–98′   Diameter: 50′–60′   Soil: 1   V–VI   ✳   !!!

Origin: Eastern and Central Europe. **Characteristics:** The common Horse Chestnut is probably the most widely distributed species of the genus *Aesculus*. It is distinguished by its height and broad, highly arched crown. The deciduous, palmately arranged leaves come in groups of 5 to 7 on one stem, range between 4′ and 10′ in length, and turn yellow in the fall. The candle-shaped blossoms appear in May or June, depending upon location, and develop prickly, poisonous fruit husks which contain the well-known chestnuts. **Growing Conditions:** *A. hippocastanum* loves sunny locations with well-drained soil and clean air. A typical urban climate which encourages premature loss of leaves does not agree with this tree. **Species and Varieties:** Since the Horse Chestnut is less well suited for the conventional home garden, smaller forms of the tree are frequently preferred for this purpose. These include *Aesculus x carnea* "Briotii." The Ruby Horse Chestnut grows to only about 40′ in height and develops a broadly arched crown. The deep red flowers appear in June and are followed by almost no fruit. Like all chestnut trees, this one prefers a deep, well-drained soil, ample water supply, and much sunlight. Another species with an interesting shape is *Aesculus parviflora*, the Bottlebrush Buckeye. As the name already indicates, this is a shrubby representative of the genus *Aesculus* which reaches a height of only 10′–13′, but which can spread out to a diameter of up to 30′. The 8″–10½″ long blossoms are terminal and appear in July and August. This shrub can tolerate a slightly shady location if it has an ample supply of water. It likes protected spots, but is, on the whole, relatively hardy. **Recommendations:** *A. hippocastanum* blends well into rural areas and in rustic settings, but it is also well suited for large landscaped gardens in suburban areas if the roots are properly provided with water and the air is good. Under these conditions, a suburban climate is completely acceptable. The branches of older Horse Chestnuts tend to break off in windy weather.

Ailanthus altissima   Tree of Heaven

Height: 65′–80′   Diameter: 30′–40′   Soil: 1   VI–VII   ✳

Origin: China. **Characteristics:** Loosely arranged crowns with large, pinnately compound leaves and ornamental fruit. **Growing Conditions:** The Tree of Heaven loves sunny locations with well-drained soil; it can survive well in urban conditions. One must keep in mind, however, that this tree tends to produce runners. **Recommendations:** *A. altissima* is highly recommended as a street or park tree and is very good for planting in larger tubs or other sizable pots. It is well suited for hot southern exposures or, with adequate precautions concerning ample supplies of air and water, for built-up areas as well, including landscaping around parking lots. On the whole, the Tree of Heaven is very ornamental and should be used more often than it is.

Alnus incana   Speckled Alder

Height: 50'–65'   Diameter: 16'–20'   Soil: 1   III   ✳

Origin: *A. incana* is indigenous to Europe and the Caucasus. **Characteristics:** This deciduous tree produces distinctly pointed, oval alternate green leaves 2"–3" in length. The male catkins of the Speckled Alder are longer than those of the European Alder (see below). **Growing Conditions:** *A. incana* likes a sunny location and also flourishes in light, sandy soil. However, the tree does not thrive in coastal areas with strong winds. **Varieties and Species:** "Aurea" does not grow any taller than 20' and has pale green leaves, yellowish shoots, and yellowish-brown catkins. *A. glutinosa,* the European Alder, has obovate leaves which are deeply lobed at the end; it grows to a height of between 65' and 80' and attains a diameter at the crown of 20' to 26'. Unlike the Speckled Alder, the European Alder also grows in damp to wet, heavy marshy soils. The species *A. glutinosa* also has a variety called "Aurea," which is not as tall and has yellowish leaves. **Recommendations:** *A. incana* can be used in larger gardens, as a landscape tree along roadways, and as a barrier against noise and dust in urban developments. It is also recommended as a pioneer plant for untreated virgin soils. Because of its modest height, the "Aurea" variety can also be used in smaller gardens.

Amelanchier canadensis   Shad Blow or Downy Serviceberry

Height: 19'–26'   Diameter: 9'–13'   Soil: 5   IV–V   ✳

Origin: North America. **Characteristics:** A deciduous tree whose new foliage ranges from silvery gray to bronze. The narrow leaves are 1½"–2" long and range in color from yellow to red in the fall. This tree is distinguished by its profuse whitish blossoms. From June onward this shrublike tree is decked with a multitude of roundish, bluish-purple edible fruits about ¼" thick. **Growing Conditions:** The Downy Serviceberry likes a sunny to slightly shady spot and soil that is well supplied with lime. It also flourishes in sandy soils if they are not too dry. **Species:** *A. laevis* with its somewhat smaller size is also a popular choice. **Recommendations:** Because of their resistance to air pollution, *A. canadensis* and other species of *Amelanchier* are very useful as solitary specimens or as group trees in planting pots, for roof gardens, apartment gardens, or parks in the inner city area. Also because of its adaptability, the Shad Blow or Downy Serviceberry is well suited for landscaping purposes in open areas. This is why these shrubby trees are so popular and so often highly recommended.

Berberis thunbergii   Japanese Barberry

Height: 3'–5'   Diameter: 20"–30"   Soil: 1–3   IV–V   ❊

Origin: Japan. **Characteristics:** Densely branched, compact woody shrub with deciduous leaves that turn a reddish color in the fall. The oval leaves are ⅝"–1¼" long. The frequently reddish-tinged blossoms hang individually in rows along the slightly pendulous boughs. The many shiny red ornamental fruits are between ⅜" and ⅝" long. **Growing Conditions:** *B. thunbergii* prefers ordinary, well-drained garden soil but it can also tolerate a somewhat acidic and heavier variety. The location can range from one with full sunlight to one with partial shade. **Recommendations:** *B. thunbergii* is pollution-resistant and can therefore be used as a hedge plant in the inner city as well as in suburban areas.

Berberis julianae   Wintergreen Barberry

Height: 7'–8'   Diameter: 5'–6½'   Soil: 1   V   ❊   E

Origin: China. **Characteristics:** An evergreen shrub with very thorny shoots. The hardy, shiny dark green elliptical leaves have sharp spines and grow to about 4" in length. The small, often reddish blossoms appear in clusters of 10 to 15 each. The oval berries are blue-black and frosted. **Growing Conditions:** *B. julianae* likes sunny to partially shady spots that are somewhat protected and have well-drained soil. **Recommendations:** Because of its small size, this shrub is well suited for many purposes in home gardens, be it as a solitary specimen or as a member of a group. It can also be planted in large tubs as well as in roof and atrium gardens. On the whole, *B. julianae* is one of the prettiest species of the evergreen *Berberis*.

Berberis thunbergii   "Atropurpurea"

Height: 3'   Diameter: 1½'–2½'   Soil: 1–3

Origin: Cultivar; that is, it was produced as a result of horticultural cross-breeding. **Characteristics:** Smaller in size than the parent plant *B. thunbergii*. The leaves are a deep brownish red from the time they appear until the time they fall, and thus are particularly ornamental. **Growing Conditions:** *B. thunbergii* "Atropurpurea" likes a sunny location with ordinary, well-drained garden soil. **Varieties and Species:** In addition to "Atropurpurea," "Atropurpurea Nana" also deserves mention. It is smaller, attaining a height of only 11½"–15¾". Neither of these varieties produces any blossoms or fruit. Other evergreen species include *B. buxifolia* "Nana" (8"–12"); *B. hookeri* (27"); and *B. x hybridogagnepainii* (6½'–10'). Deciduous forms include *B. aggregata* (3'–5') and *B. x ottawensis* "Superba," (6½'). **Recommendations:** Like their parent plant, the varieties "Atropurpurea" and "Atropurpurea Nana" are pollution-resistant and can be shaped into hedges. Moreover, "Atropurpurea Nana" is well suited for barrier hedges and rock gardens.

24

Betula pendula   European Birch, White Birch

Height: 65'   Diameter: 20'–26'   Soil: 1–3   IV–V   ❋

Origin: *B. pendula* (synonym *B. verrucosa*) is indigenous to all of Europe and Asia Minor. **Characteristics:** The European Birch has a loosely shaped crown that tends to hang over slightly with age and whose slender lateral branches hang downward. The designation *pendula* (i.e., hanging) is a direct reference to this characteristic. The branches and the upper portion of the trunk are covered with a predominantly white bark. The lower portion of the trunk is black and cracked. **Growing Conditions:** *B. pendula* needs a bright, sunny spot and makes few demands on the soil; sandy, poor soils, or slightly acidic ones are perfectly acceptable. **Varieties and Species:** In keeping with its name, "Gracilis" has a graceful appearance; it grows to a height of only 16'–20'. "Tristis" is taller and has long, weeping pendulous side branches. "Youngii" is a smaller weeping variety with a rounded crown and branches that hang down to the ground in a wide, bell-like shape. "Fastigiata" has a columnar shape and attains a height of 50'. "Purpurea" develops brownish-red leaves that later turn to a greenish bronze. In addition to the widely distributed European Birch, there are other species of this tree that deserve mentioning. *B. nigra,* the River Birch, indigenous to the United States, is a single- or multiple-trunked tree or large shrub with a loosely shaped crown; it grows to a height of 50'–65' and a diameter of 13'–16'. It likes sunny spots and ordinary to lighter, somewhat acidic soils. *B. pubescens,* also called the Marsh Birch, is indigenous to Europe and grows to 65' in height and 32'–50' in diameter; it tolerates boglike acidic soil with a good supply of water.
Recommendations: The European Birch is a popular tree for gardens, parks, and streets, and is also well suited for planting in poor, relatively dry soil. The smaller pendular and columnar forms blend well in home gardens. Because of their smaller size, the varieties "Gracilis" and "Youngii" are preferred for this purpose, although "Gracilis" is less easily available. "Youngii" is frequently found in cemeteries, but this should not deter anyone from featuring it on private property as part of a field flower garden or a planted corner with a similar emphasis.

Buddleia alternifolia   Fountain Buddleia

Height: 10'   Diameter: 13'–16'   Soil: 2–1   VI

Origin: China. **Characteristics:** *B. alternifolia* is distinguished by a flat, globose shape with long, slender overhanging lateral branches. The pale green deciduous leaves are lanceolate and about 1" in length. *B. alternifolia* blooms in June on the previous year's growth; hence any pruning—if even necessary in the first place—should only be done after the bloom. The small tubular blossoms are arranged in clusters on the upper side of the pendulous branches and are very fragrant. **Growing Conditions:** Required is a sunny, protected location with light to medium heavy soil and ample moisture without any standing water. **Species and Varieties:** In addition to the highly recommended *B. alternifolia*, which is still relatively sparsely distributed, there is a wide variety of choices among the species, including *B. davidii*, the Orange-Eye Butterflybush, which grows to a height of 10'–16' and a diameter of 10'–13'. The overhanging side shoots produce terminal flower clusters with fragrant, tubular individual blossoms. This species needs a sunny location and relatively light soil. *B. davidii* "Black Night" is dark violet; "Empire Blue," blue-violet; "Fascination," pink; "Ile de France," blue-violet; "Purple Prince," reddish violet; "Royal Red," purplish red; "White Profusion," white. **Recommendations:** *B. alternifolia* has a particularly ornamental effect as a solitary specimen on a lawn. In this setting, its typical growth pattern is displayed to great advantage. The narrow-leafed Orange-Eye Butterflybush blends in well with conifers. Large needle trees frequently make a very decorative background for *B. alternifolia*.

Buxus sempervirens   Common Box

Height: 20'–26'   Diameter: 16'–20'   Soil: 5–2   E

Origin: Mediterranean regions, Caucasus. **Characteristics:** *B. sempervirens* forms treelike shrubs with shiny red evergreen leaves 1¼"–2" long. **Growing Conditions:** The Common Box likes a well-drained limestone soil and tolerates shade. **Recommendations:** Since it also tolerates pruning very well, *B. sempervirens* is an excellent choice for a hedge plant or for the construction of low enclosures and borders.

Callicarpa bodinieri   Bodinier Beautyberry

Height: 6½'–10'   Diameter: 6½'   Soil: 1–5   VII   ❄

Origin: Western China. **Characteristics:** *C. bodinieri* is a deciduous shrub that blooms in midsummer. The pale green leaves become colorful in the fall when the violet berry-shaped fruit, each the size of a peppercorn, cluster in dense cymes along the boughs of this upright plant. It is somewhat sensitive to cold and can freeze to the ground in rugged locations during severe winters. As a rule, however, this shrub revives again in spring after removal of the dead branches. **Growing Conditions:** A protected spot with ordinary garden soil is required. In more rugged locations it is a good idea to provide some sort of winter protection. **Varieties:** "Profusion" is distinguished by a rich production of fruit with each individual piece relatively large in size. The variety *C. bodinieri var. giraldii* (illustration above) is particularly hardy and therefore widely distributed. **Recommendations:** *C. bodinieri* works well when planted in front of larger woody plants, and the cuttings can be used for very attractive vase arrangements.

Carpinus betulus   European Hornbeam

Height: 50'–65'   Diameter: 33'–39'   Soil: 1–5   V   ❄

Origin: Indigenous to regions ranging from Europe to Iran. **Characteristics:** As a tree, *C. betulus* is characterized by a high top and smooth gray bark which looks swollen in places as it ages. The pointed oval leaves are sharply cut and denticulated; they turn yellow in the fall and brown thereafter on those varieties with clinging leaves. Blossoms and fruit (nuts with bracteoles) are insignificant. **Growing Conditions:** *C. betulus* likes a rather moist soil rich in humus and lime and, because of its horizontally running shallow roots, it can tolerate a relatively high level of ground water. **Varieties:** "Fastigiata" with a columnar shape; "Purpurea" with at first brownish, then later green leaves and small size; "Quercifolia" with leaves that resemble those of an oak tree. **Recommendations:** The Hornbeam is a hardy and densely growing woody plant. It needs little care and can thus be used for a variety of purposes in an open landscape. It makes a good windscreen, for example, and can be featured both as a solitary specimen, in groups, or in rows. Moreover, the Hornbeam is in popular demand as a hedge plant because it tolerates shearing and trimming and tends to branch out well where it was cut. If you plan to use the Hornbeam as a hedge, it is especially important to buy a specimen that is equally and well trimmed from bottom to top. It pays to spend a little more in the beginning to ensure an even and dense hedge later on. It is also important to ascertain whether the autumn leaves cling to the bush or whether they fall off prematurely. If privacy is a high priority, you should choose a plant that does not lose its leaves early. A good supply of water and appropriate nutrients are also important for the continued flourishing of this hedge.

Cedrus deodara   Deodar Cedar

Height: 65'   Diameter: 20'–26'   Soil: 1

Origin: Himalayan Mountains. **Characteristics:** This conifer is generally distinguished by its pyramidal shape in horizontal lateral branches and pendulous boughs. The top shoot, too, usually droops a bit to one side. Because of its somewhat irregular growth pattern, particularly in the early years, this conifer has a very elegant appearance. In their early stages the needles are frequently a bluish-green color and change with age into a deep dark green. **Growing Conditions:** Under central European climatic conditions, *C. deodara* needs a protected habitat with a deep, sufficiently moist soil rich in nutrients and free of standing water. Another requirement is a large expanse of surrounding space so that this conifer can spread out as it wishes. **Varieties and Species:** "Aurea" sets young shoots with yellow needles which later take on a greenish tinge. "Verticilata Glauca" grows extremely straight and has gray-green needles. Another species very well suited for inclusion in large gardens or parks with gentler surroundings is *C. atlantica*, the Atlas Cedar, which can develop its own typical growth patterns if given enough room: this species can attain a height of 100'–130' and a diameter of 20'–26'. It makes the same claims on soil as does the Deodar Cedar. *C. atlantica* "Aurea," on the other hand, grows into small trees 10'–16' tall with yellowish-green needles. *C. atlantica* "Glauca" has needles ranging in color from blue-green to silver-gray and has a very loose and attractive shape. *C. libani*, the Cedar of Lebanon, grows slowly in its younger years and eventually attains its ultimately wide, pyramidal shape. It can attain a height of 80'–130' and a diameter of 33'–39'. **Recommendations:** The Deodar Cedar is well suited for larger gardens and landscapes if it is provided with a protected and sufficiently large location.

Cercidiphyllum japonicum   Katsura Tree

Height: 16′–33′   Diameter: 16′–26′   Soil: 1   IV

Origin: This lovely tree is indigenous to Japan. **Characteristics:** As a rule, *C. japonicum* forms a multi-trunked tree with several rather boldly upward-growing main branches and somewhat overhanging, slender lateral branches and boughs. The inconspicuous reddish blossoms smell like gingerbread. The deciduous leaves have a flattened heart shape. They are the color of bronze when they first emerge, and range from yellow to red in the fall. They, too, give off the typical gingerbread scent. **Growing Conditions:** *C. japonicum* is fairly sensitive to cold during its sprouting period and for this reason ought to be given a protected spot. Moreover, this tree needs a sunny location for its optimal development, and a place where it can expand as it wishes. The soil has to be sufficiently moist, free from standing water, and rich in nutrients. **Recommendations:** *C. japonicum* is an elegant ornamental tree that is well suited for larger gardens and parks. In such a setting it is very attractive if it is planted at a sufficient distance from other large trees. On the whole, it deserves more attention than it has thus far enjoyed because, in addition to its charming appearance, it has the advantage of modest height and thus retains relatively small dimensions for a considerable length of time.

Chaenomeles japonica   Japanese Quince

Height: 3½′   Diameter: 3½′   Soil: 1   IV–V   ✳

Origin: Japan. **Characteristics:** *C. japonica* forms small broad shrubs with widely spreading branches, hardy, shiny dark green leaves, and ornamental, radiant blossoms. Dense, aromatic, applelike fruits 1″–2″ in size develop out of the blossoms. **Growing Conditions:** *C. japonica* likes bright, sunny situations with ordinary, well-drained soil. **Varieties and Species:** "Crimson and Gold" as well as "Simonii" are dark red and only 1½′–3′ tall. Between 3′ and 5′ in height are "K. Ramcke," vermilion; "Elly Mossel," fiery red; "Fascination," scarlet; "Firedance," blood red; "Hollandia," scarlet; "Nicoline," scarlet with large blossoms; "Nivalis," white. Those varieties that attain a height of 6½′ include "Ernst Finken," luminescent red, and "Versicolor Lutescens," light pink. *C. speciosa* blooms from April to June and also produces fruit. As in the case of *C. japonica,* the blossoms, which are larger and appear in smaller clusters, form on the previous year's growth. This thorny, squarrose shrub grows up to 6½′ tall and wide. *C. speciosa* "Brilliant" is deep red and blooms profusely. **Recommendations:** Suitable for low, flowering hedges in a trimmed or untrimmed state. It has many uses as a solitary specimen or group plant, especially in home gardens. Individual branches make charming displays in a vase; before putting them in, however, you should pound or cut the shoots lengthwise near the end. Radical trimming should be avoided in the case of both species of *Chaenomeles* as well as in hedges, for this will reduce the number of blossoms in the following year.

Chamaecyparis lawsoniana   Lawson False Cypress

Height: 50'–66'   Diameter: 16'   Soil: 1   V   ❄   E

Origin: California. **Characteristics:** A pointed pyramidal tree with reddish male blossoms and scalelike leaves arranged in rows. **Growing Conditions:** Sufficiently moist humus or slightly marshy soil; unsuited for the inner city environment. **Varieties:** The following varieties attain a height of 16'–33': "Alumii," dark green, bluish, and frosted; "Columnaris," narrow, columnar, blue-green; "Erecta Viridis," bright green, columnar; "Fraseri," similar to "Alumii" but darker. 6½'–10' in height are "Elwoodii," cone-shaped, blue-green; other cone-shaped dwarf varieties include "Forsteckensis" and "Minima Glauca." **Recommendations:** The dwarf varieties are particularly suited for rock gardens, while the larger varieties can be used wherever accent through shape and color is desirable.

Chamaecyparis nootkatensis   Nootka False Cypress

Height: 50'   Diameter: 16'–20'   Soil: 1   E

Origin: Western North America. **Characteristics:** This hardy tree grows to a height of 130' in its native habitat. It is distinguished by a slender, pyramidal shape. The branches are yellowish and somewhat square, and have dark green, scaly foliage. **Growing Conditions:** The ornamental value of this tree can only unfold in open space. An ordinary garden soil meets all the requirements. **Varieties:** "Pendula" (illustration upper right) with downward hanging lateral branches, 16'–33' tall, very popular. "Flauca," bluish and frosted. **Recommendations:** *C. nootkatensis* is best suited for larger gardens and parks; "Pendula" can also be used for smaller garden plots.

Chamaecyparis obtusa   Hinoki False Cypress

Height: 33'–50'   Diameter: 13'–16'   Soil: 1   E

Origin: Japan. **Characteristics:** Modest height. **Growing Conditions:** Ordinary garden soil. **Varieties:** "Nana Gracilis" (illustration lower left) is a very popular form with a pyramidal shape, up to 6½' tall; "Crippsii," 10'–16', golden yellow and broad; "Filicoides," fernlike, 5'; "Pygmaea," bluish green, broadly globose. **Recommendations:** Suitable for small home gardens.

Chamaecyparis pisifera   Sawara False Cypress

Height: 66'   Diameter: 16'   Soil: 1   E

Origin: Japan. **Characteristics:** Low growth. **Growing Conditions:** Ordinary garden soil. **Varieties:** "Plumosa aurea" with feathery foliage; "Filifera Nana" with a low growth and long, outstretched threadlike shoots; "Boulevard," light blue-green. **Recommendations:** See *C. obtusa*.

Colutea arborescens   Bladder Senna

Height: 10'   Diameter: 10'   Soil: 1–2   VII–VIII   ✳

Origin: Mediterranean region. **Characteristics:** This expansive shrub belongs to the *Leguminosae* family. Its branches are covered with gray bark and produce yellow to brownish blossoms from July to August. These are followed by large green blistered fruit husks which later turn a reddish brown. The shrub is deciduous and covered with unpaired penna leaves. On the whole, this shrub is categorized as hardy and undemanding and tolerates even radical pruning. **Growing Conditions:** *C. arborescens* grows in ordinary garden soil as well as in poor, sandy soil. Even alkaline soils are acceptable. In either case this plant can also tolerate occasional dry spells. **Species:** *Colutea x media* is a cross between *C. arborescens* and *C. orientalis* and grows to a height of 6½'–10'. The blossoms range from orange to bluish yellow and appear during the summer. After blooming this shrub also produces bladderlike seed pods. *C. orientalis* only grows to 6½', but makes up in width what it lacks in height. The reddish-brown blossoms appear from June to September and are followed by fruit. **Recommendations:** Because of its hardiness, *C. arborescens* is exceptionally well suited as a pioneer plant in untreated soil or in areas with poor soil conditions and intense sunshine. Moreover, the Bladder Senna can be used to great advantage to fill in the gaps between other growing trees and shrubs.

Cornus mas   Cornelian Cherry

Height: 16'–20'   Diameter: 10'–16'   Soil: 1–5   III–IV   ✳

Origin: *C. mas* is indigenous to Central Europe and has become naturalized in the Caucasus and Asia Minor. **Characteristics:** It is usually found in the form of a multi-trunked large shrub with upright main branches and somewhat squarrose side shoots. The deciduous leaves are elliptical and 2"–4" long. Profuse small yellow blossoms appear on older branches in March and April, and in the summer these develop into edible barrel-shaped shiny red fruits about ¾" long. **Growing Conditions:** *C. mas* is an adaptable shrub that prefers ordinary garden soil but also flourishes in poor, alkaline soils. **Species and Varieties:** In addition to the widely distributed *C. mas*, there are also other species and other varieties with ornamental potential. *C. alba* "Marginata Elegans," 6½' tall, with whitish deciduous leaves and reddish autumnal coloration. This variety loves warm, sunny locations. *C. alba* "Sibirica" is distinguished by coral red shoots that lend color to the garden in winter, 6½' tall. *C. alba* "Spaethii" also grows to a height of 6½' and produces variegated leaves with yellow markings. *C. florida* is characterized by a height of 20'–26' and red autumnal coloration. **Recommendations:** Because of its adaptability, *C. mas* has many applications, including use as a solitary specimen, in groups, as a hedge, or in large tubs. It also flourishes in an urban environment.

Corylus avellana European Hazel

Height: 16'   Diameter: 13'–16'   Soil: 1   II–III   *

Origin: Europe. **Characteristics:** As a rule, the hazelnut grows as a large multi-branched shrub with diagonal or horizontal lateral shoots. The deciduous leaves have a rounded heart shape and are slightly pointed and toothed. The hazelnut is monoecious; in this case, the male blossoms appear in the form of the well-known catkins, while the plain female blossoms remain more in the inner portions of the same bush. This shrub is hardy and pollution-resistant. In order to obtain fruit, different varieties ought to be planted. **Growing Conditions:** The hazelnut does not make any particular claims, but it does like deep, nutrient-containing soil and can tolerate some shade as well. **Varieties and Species:** "Aurea" produces yellow leaves in spring. "Contorta" (illustration top) grows much lower (6½'–8') and produces corkscrewlike twisted twigs which lend it its unique appearance. "Rote Zellernuss" is a tall, large shrub that produces pleasant-tasting nuts in September; its leaves are reddish brown. In addition to these bushy varieties, there is C. colurna, the Turkish Filbert, which can attain a height of 66' and whose crown regularly renews itself on top. The male catkins grow to a length of 4"–5", and the fruits appear in clusters. The Turkish Filbert does not need much attention and is resistant to the ravages of an urban environment. **Recommendations:** The normal shrub form of the hazelnut can be planted in parks between widely separated large trees; it can also be used as a windscreen with the added advantage of fruit, or as a solitary specimen in smaller to medium-sized gardens. The same holds true for "Rote Zellernuss." C. avellana "Contorta" is usually planted in sunny, prominent places and can have a nicely ornamental effect. The Turkish Filbert makes a good solitary specimen or street tree. It must be mentioned, however, that all varieties of hazelnut are among the first plants to produce significant amounts of pollen.

Cotinus coggygria Smoketree

Height: 6½'–13'   Diameter: 6½'–10'   Soil: 1–5   VI–VII   *

Origin: Mediterranean region to the Near East. **Characteristics:** C. coggygria grows in the form of expansive bushes with deciduous elliptical entire leaves that are clearly veined and which range in color from orange to red in the fall. The insignificant individual blossoms are yellowish green (illustration lower right) and they appear in June and July on the ends of long, hairy, featherlike panicles that can reach about 8" in length. The blossoms frequently fall unfertilized, but the fruits grow by producing hairlike appendages which lend the plant its wiglike appearance. **Growing Conditions:** Warm, alkaline soil in full direct sunlight. **Varieties:** "Rubrifolia" (illustration lower left) with strikingly dark purple leaves. "Red Beauty" with particularly large leaves that start off purplish red and then turn dark red. "Royal Purple," a vigorous variety with dark leaves. **Recommendations:** This hardy shrub can be used for many purposes and is highly recommended.

Cotoneaster horizontalis   Rock Spray

Height: 1½'–10'   Diameter: 10'   Soil: 1   VI   ✳

Origin: Western China, Szechuan. **Characteristics:** *C. horizontalis* is probably the most popular variety of *Cotoneaster*. It is distinguished by a squarrose shape and a typically flat arrangement of lateral branches. When planted close to walls, this shrub braces itself against the wall and can thus climb to a height of 10'. The small (⅙"–¾"), shiny, oval pointed leaves grow very close together and turn a reddish color before falling in late autumn. The June bloom ranges from white to pale pink and is followed by a profuse covering of berrylike red fruit which lends *C. horizontalis* its striking appearance. This shrub is pollution-resistant, but it can suffer under severe winter weather. **Growing Conditions:** *C. horizontalis* does not require any unusual soil conditions. **Varieties:** "Robusta" is characterized by a greater resistance to frost. **Recommendations:** *C. horizontalis* can be used for many purposes, as a solitary specimen or group plant, for slopes, rock gardens, or in large planting tubs.

Cotoneaster dammeri   Bearberry Cotoneaster

Height: 6"–8"   Soil: 1   VI   ✳   E

Origin: China and Szechuan. **Characteristics:** With lateral branches that lie on the ground and root, *C. dammeri* is distinguished by its very low height. It has a tendency to form an overhang on walls. The evergreen leaves are oval and ½"–¾" long. The white blossoms in June are followed by radiant red fruits. **Growing Conditions:** *C. dammeri* likes a sunny location with soil that is not too dry, but it can also tolerate shade. Trimming is possible. **Varieties:** "Coral Beauty" with a profusion of ornamental fruit and particular resistance to winter weather. "Major" and "Stockholm" grow more vigorously and are somewhat taller. **Recommendations:** *C. dammeri* is currently considered an especially prized and versatile ground cover.

Cotoneaster x watereri

Height: 10'–13'   Diameter: 13'   Soil: 1   VI   ✳

Origin: Hybrid. **Characteristics:** *C. x watereri* is a representative of the many hybrids of *Cotoneaster*. It forms large shrubs with pendulous branches. The dull green leaves, 2¾"–4" in length, are frequently evergreen. In order to bear abundant fruit, the blossoms, which appear in the form of white cymes, need a partner bush. **Growing Conditions:** No particular requirements; it can even bear some shade. **Species:** *Cotoneaster dielsianus*, 6½' in height, grows freely and can be used for hedges. *C. salicifolius*, 13' tall, has wide, pendulous side shoots. *C. multiflorus*, particularly profuse in bloom, is 13' high and provides an excellent plant for a bee and butterfly garden. **Recommendations:** *C. x watereri* is best used as a solitary specimen.

Crataegus laevigata   English Hawthorn

Height: 13′–16′   Diameter: 6½′–10′   Soil: 1–5   V–VI   ✳

Origin: *C. laevigata* is indigenous to Europe and North Africa. **Characteristics:** This hardy and pollution-resistant woody plant has considerable ornamental value. It can be purchased both in shrub and tree form. The trees have relatively small tops. The individual white blossoms are between ⅜″ and ⅝″ in diameter and bloom in corymb panicles. These later develop into the scarlet fruit, which provides the plant's particular ornamental value. The deciduous leaves turn yellow in fall. **Growing Conditions:** The English Hawthorn prefers a sunny location with relatively light to medium-heavy alkaline soil. **Varieties and Species:** "Alboplena," broad and expansive with double white blossoms that fade to a pinkish color. "Gireoudii," with variegated leaves and large fruits. "Paul Scarlet," very popular as a small tree suitable for gardens, paths, and streets. "Rubra Plena," fairly widely distributed variety with double carmine red blossoms. Also recommended is *C. monogyna*, a shrub 16′–26′ in height, and available in tree form as well. The white blossoms appear in corymb form in May; these are followed by red fruits which, in contrast to *C. laevigata*, have only a single stone. **Recommendations:** As a shrub or a tree, *C. laevigata* is well suited for planting in smaller areas, especially in home gardens, and as a street tree along a path or a road. The related species *C. monogyna* can be used for these same purposes, as well as be trimmed to a hedge.

Cytisus x praecox   Warminster Broom

Height: 6½′   Diameter: 6½′   Soil: 1   IV–V   !!!

Origin: *C. x praecox* was cultivated by crossing *C. multiflorus* with *C. purgans*. Although both parent plants are indigenous to the Mediterranean region and are hardly ever found north of the Alps, *C. x praecox* can tolerate a somewhat more severe climate. **Characteristics:** *C. x praecox* is distinguished by its especially charming shape and its elegantly overhanging flowers. The lobed deciduous leaves are lanceolate, ⅜″–⅝″ long. The profusion of yellow blossoms emerges from the previous year's shoots and is very fragrant. **Growing Conditions:** The only requirements are a sunny spot and well-drained soil. **Varieties and Species:** "Allgold" is easily available and is recommended. "Gold Spear" blooms a deep yellow. Among the new *Cytisus* hybrids, the Dutch cultivars "Hollandia" and "Zeelandia" can be considered successful and are already available in many places. Hardier than *C. x praecox* is *Cytisus scoparius*, commonly called Scotch Broom. **Recommendations:** *C. x praecox* works well in gardens with a wilderness look, as, for example, in field flower gardens, rock gardens, or near conifers. *C. scoparius* can also be used for landscapes with extensive care but in the drier spots. Since some *Cytisus* species have difficulty in growing, you should purchase only those plants with root balls. Furthermore, because they are poisonous, these plants should not be planted where children play.

Daphne mezereum February Daphne

Height: 3'	Diameter: 2'–2½'	Soil: 4–5	III–IV	❄	!!!

Origin: *D. mezereum* is indigenous to Europe, Asia Minor, and the Caucasus as far east as Siberia. **Characteristics:** Daphne forms shrubs with rounded tops about 3' tall. The bloom, which varies according to its location and weather conditions, appears in March or April, is very fragrant and carmine red. The individual tubular blossoms are distributed in discrete bunches along the boughs. The deciduous leaves appear after the first full bloom; they are 1½'–3" long, light green, and narrowly oval in shape. This shrub is pollution-resistant and winter-hardy. As a rule, it does not need any pruning. A word of caution: the red fruits of *D. mezereum* are very poisonous. **Growing Conditions:** *Daphne* likes a well-drained and sufficiently moist soil that contains humus and lime. Since it is a natural underbrush, it tolerates shade but can also thrive in the sun. **Varieties and Species:** "Alba" blooms white and produces yellow fruits. "Ruby Glow" has large, dark purplish-red blossoms and is highly recommended. Another ornamental but somewhat sensitive species is *D. cneorum*. This equally poisonous plant is indigenous to Central and Southern Europe and grows to a height of about 1'. It has a creeping growth, and carmine red blossoms in May and June. **Recommendations:** *D. mezereum* can stand alone or be planted in small groups together with other early bloomers. It is a good idea to arrange plants such as these as close as possible to the house. Since Daphne is very poisonous, it should not be planted where children might come in contact with it. *D. cneorum* makes a good bolster in rock gardens.

Deutzia gracilis Slender Deutzia

Height: 1½'–3'	Diameter: 1½'–2'	Soil: 1	V–VI

Origin: Japan. **Characteristics:** *D. gracilis* grows into small shrubs with long (1¼"–2½") lanceolate deciduous leaves that are lobed and taper to a point. The pure white blossoms appear in May and June in upright clusters. This shrub blooms profusely and is pollution-resistant. **Growing Conditions:** *D. gracilis* does not need any special attention as far as soil is concerned and can tolerate slight shade. **Species and Varieties:** *D. x lemoinei* grows upright and loose, attains a height of about 6½', and produces white blossoms in July. "Mont Rose" has pink blossoms. *D. x magnifica* grows straight upward to a height of 10'–13'; its profuse, double pure white blossoms appear in the form of round corymb panicles in May and June. *D. x rosea* is only 3' high and produces large, ¾" pink blossoms in June which consist of loose panicles and are white on the inside. *D. scabra* is about 10' tall and blooms in June and July. *D. scabra* "Plena" sets double pink blossoms. All of these species and varieties are distinguished by their adaptability to soil conditions; they are very versatile. **Recommendations:** *D. gracilis* is suited for smaller gardens as a solitary specimen or as a member of a group as well as for loose flowering hedges. Daphne can also be forced.

Euonymus europaeus   European Spindletree

Height: 13′–16′   Diameter: 10′   Soil: 1   V   ✳   !!!

Origin: Europe, but it can be found as far as Western Asia. **Characteristics:** This woody plant usually comes in shrub form, but there is also a tree form; both have small cork wings on their shoots. The long deciduous leaves are oval and taper to a point; in the fall they range in color from orange to reddish. The inconspicuous yellowish-green blossoms appear in May and produce the actual ornament of this hardy plant, the four-lobed orange fruits that hang down in bunches and explode after a while to expose the yellow seeds. These seeds are poisonous. The Spindletree is hardy and resistant to pollution, but its tender young shoots are susceptible to aphids. **Growing Conditions:** *E. europaeus* makes no special demands as far as soil is concerned and it can tolerate sun as well as partial shade. **Species and Varieties:** *E. alatus* is indigenous to Northeast Asia and Central China. It is a slowly growing bush that takes a long time to attain a height of 7′–10′. Blossoms and fruit are insignificant. The ornamental value of this special plant lies in its pronounced wing-shaped cork bands and in its glorious carmine red autumn coloration. This species is pollution-resistant and is well suited for smaller gardens. *E. fortunei* is an evergreen clinging vine. "Gracilis" and "Silver Gem" have yellowish-white variegated leaves and grow more slowly than the green form. *E. fortunei* works well as a solitary specimen or as a ground cover in larger areas and for covering low walls, etc. Caution! *E. fortunei* is also poisonous. **Recommendations:** *E. europaeus* can stand alone or be planted in groups. Because of the toxicity of its seeds, however, the Spindletree should be planted only in places inaccessible to children.

Forsythia x intermedia   Border Forsythia

Height: 6½′–10′   Diameter: 6½′–10′   Soil: 1   IV–V

Origin: *F. x intermedia* resulted from crossing *F. viridissima* with *F. suspensa*. **Characteristics:** *F. x intermedia* grows in the form of a shrub whose main branches stand fairly straight up while the lateral branches in older plants tend to hang over a bit. The deciduous leaves are ovate-lanceolate and toothed, and the blossoms, which emerge from the previous year's growth, are dense and yellow. **Growing Conditions:** An ordinary garden soil without clumps, a great deal of sunlight, and no standing water are desirable. **Varieties and Species:** At the moment, "Lynwood" is considered the best variety because of its profuse blossoms and the intensity of its color. However, the older varieties "Spectabilis" as well as "Spring Glory" are also recommended. *F. suspensa* is a shrub which grows to a height of 10′ with yellow blossoms on widely arching lateral branches. **Recommendations:** *Forsythia* is a hardy, versatile woody plant. It is very attractive in combination with red bloomers, such as tulips or winter currants.

Hamamelis japonica   Japanese Witch Hazel

Height: 16′   Diameter: 10′–13′   Soil: 1–3   I–III

Origin: Japan. **Characteristics:** This shrub is distinguished by its upright and unconstricted appearance. Its leaves can grow to a length of 4″ and resemble those of the hazelnut. The blossoms start appearing on bald wood as early as January. They bloom in bunches of 3 or more and are distinguished by yellow threadlike petals, ¾″ long, and a reddish-brown calyx. *H. japonica* and the other *Hamamelis* species need no pruning, but they can be cut for display in vases. This shrub is pollution-resistant and can also be forced indoors. **Growing Conditions:** Like its related species, *H. japonica* needs a medium-heavy to heavy, well-drained soil and an open, sunny to partially shady location. **Varieties and Species:** Worth mentioning is ''Zuccarina'' that blooms rather late with greenish-yellow blossoms. *H. mollis* is indigenous to China and when mature reaches a height of about 16′. It develops a cone-shaped crown and produces yellow blossoms during the period between January and March. ''Brevipetala'' is only about 10′ tall and sets small, yellowish-orange blossoms in January and February. ''Pallida'' produces larger, greenish-yellow blossoms that have a pleasant fragrance. **Recommendations:** Because it blooms so early and has such an unusual appearance, *H. japonica*, like the other species, needs a place of its own in home gardens, in parks, or as the center of attraction in large flower pots. Other species of *Hamamelis* can also be used in Japanese gardens.

Hippophae rhamnoides   Common Sea Buckthorn

Height: 23′   Diameter: 10′   Soil: 2   III–IV

Origin: *H. rhamnoides* is indigenous to Western and Eastern Asia, and has become naturalized in the Caucasus and in Europe. **Characteristics:** *H. rhamnoides* is distinguished by its squarrose appearance and its thorny lateral branches. Another typical characteristic is the production of runners, which under certain circumstances may prove to be unwelcome in some gardens. This shrub is covered with 2″–2¾″, narrow, lance-shaped deciduous leaves, both sides of which are covered with small scales. *H. rhamnoides* is dioecious; that is, there are separate male and female plants and both have to be present for the bush to produce its profuse quantities of reddish-orange fruit, which, by the way, are high in vitamin C content. **Growing Conditions:** This shrub needs a lot of direct sunlight. It thrives in medium heavy soil, but prefers sandy soils. **Recommendations:** In keeping with its natural habitat and the fact that its leaves are protected against evaporation, *H. rhamnoides* is especially well suited for drier, windy positions. This is why landscape gardeners use it for protecting coastline dunes against erosion. In the garden this plant can be successfully employed in locations with a southern exposure and on embankments, for such uses exploit its tendency to produce runners. The Common Sea Buckthorn is particularly prized because of its bizarre appearance and its striking fruits.

Hydrangea paniculata   Panicle Hydrangea

Height: 6½'–9'   Diameter: 5'–6½'   Soil: 4   VIII

Origin: China and Japan. **Characteristics:** *H. paniculata* forms wide round shrubs with terminal flowers. The deciduous leaves are long and oval, tapering to a point at the end. They range in length from 4" to 6". The creamy white blossoms are arranged in the form of pyramidal clusters and can attain a length of up to 10". They begin to appear during July, come into full bloom in August, and then die away during September and October. The individual blossoms are distinguished by a particularly long life on the bush. Since they appear on the current year's growth, unlike *H. macrophylla, H. paniculata* can tolerate a fairly radical cutting back in the winter to a height of just a few centimeters above ground. *H. paniculata* is robust and winter hardy. **Growing Conditions:** *H. paniculata* needs a soil rich in humus and an abundant water supply. It likes partial shade but can also tolerate a sunny location if it is sufficiently moist. **Varieties:** "Grandiflora" is the most successful variety and produces blossoms that are slightly tinged with pink. "Praecox" blooms 4 to 6 weeks earlier and remains lower. **Species:** *H. macrophylla* is the widely distributed House Hydrangea. It can survive the winter outside if it is planted in protected spots with favorable climatic conditions. It likes partial shade and acidic soils rich in humus. It is also good to provide some sort of winter protection. The House Hydrangea should not be cut back in the winter, for the blossoms appear on the previous year's shoots. *H. arborescens* grows into expansive bushes between 3' and 10' tall and produces ornamental, terminal greenish-white flowers from July to September. **Recommendations:** *H. paniculata* is a highly versatile plant as long as its habitat requirements are kept in mind. It is very attractive when planted as part of a group on a larger lawn.

Hypericum calycinum   St. John's Wort, Aaronsbeard

Height: approx. 1'   Soil: 3–1   VI–IX   E

Origin: Southeast Europe and Asia Minor. **Characteristics:** *H. calycinum* is a low-growing, semievergreen shrub that spreads out flat over the ground. Its sturdy but dull deep green leaves are oval and opposite, and can grow to between 2" and 3" in length. The blossoms appear at the end of June and continue to September on the ends of the current year's growth. They are an iridescent yellow, have a diameter of about 2"–2¾", and are distinguished by a bunch of yellow filaments with reddish tips. St. John's Wort can be cut back almost to the ground toward the end of winter. **Growing Conditions:** Ordinary to light soils in sunny to partially shady locations are satisfactory. **Species and Varieties:** Of the many species of *Hypericum,* special mention should be made of *H. patulum,* which grows to a height of 3'–5'. *H. patulum* "Hidcote Gold" is also recommended. **Recommendations:** Because of its relatively low height and its habit of spreading out, this woody plant is a popular ground cover.

Juniperus communis   Common Juniper

Height: 16'   Diameter: 3'–6½'   Soil: 3–1   ✳   E

Origin: *J. communis* (illustration upper left) grows wild in Europe, Northern Asia, North Africa, and North America. **Characteristics:** The common juniper tree is dioecious (individual male and female plants). The fruit—the well-known juniper berries—appear only if both partners are present. If the soil is good, this tree assumes a columnar shape, but in poorer soils it grows wider. **Growing Conditions:** Sunny spots in ordinary to poor soil. **Varieties:** "Depressa Aurea" with a vaselike shape and golden yellow tips on its shoots. "Hibernica" with a narrow, columnar shape, blue-green. "Hornibrookii," green, but turning brownish in winter, low with a creeping growth pattern and horizontal branches. "Pyramidalis" with a wide shape and several peaks, bluish gray-green. "Repanda," a low, creeping dwarf shrub with a height of 12" and a diameter of 5'; the upper side of the needles have a silvery stripe. "Suecica," narrow, columnar, with blue-green needles. **Recommendations:** Because of its diversity of shapes, the individual varieties of *J. communis* have many uses in smaller gardens.

Juniperus chinensis   Japanese Garden Juniper

Height: 3'–10'   Diameter: 3'–10'   Soil: 1   E   !!!

Origin: China. **Characteristics:** Dioecious plants whose male forms grow in columnar shape while the female forms are wider and have overhanging branches. On the whole a hardy, versatile shrub. **Growing Conditions:** A sunny to partially shady location, moist to medium-heavy soil. **Varieties and Species:** "Pfitzeriana" (illustration below) is a mighty shrub with outspread branches and dark green, scaley needles. "Pfitzeriana Aurea" has the same shape but a more modest height and remains a constant greenish gold. "Pfitzeriana Compacta," with gray-green needles; it is lower but also denser and more compact than the other two. "Blaauw" grows into wide columns about 6½' tall and has blue-green needles. "Hetzii," tall and hardy, blue-green in color. "Obelisk," blue-green, wide columns. "Plumosa," a wide, expansive shrub with featherlike green needles; it can reach a height of 5'. Related *Juniperus* species: *J. horizontalis,* a creeping form about 12" tall which slowly attains its ultimate height of 8'–10'. *J. sabina* grows to 6½'–10' tall, partially on the ground, partially erect. *J. squamata* is best known in the form of "Meyeri," which has blue-green needles and can reach a height of 5'–6½'; the important thing to remember about this plant is that it needs a lot of water, because without it it tends to turn brown from the inside out. *J. virginiana* (illustration upper right) has a columnar to cone-shaped appearance. **Recommendations:** Again because of the differing shapes, this woody plant is versatile and suitable for any type of garden.

Kerria japonica Kerria

Height: 5′–6½′   Diameter: 3′–5′   Soil: 1   V–IX

Origin: Eastern Asia. **Characteristics:** While *K. japonica,* the original form, only grows 3′ tall, the garden varieties attain a height of 5′–6½′. Moreover, the original form produces runners. The typically yellow buttercup blossoms grow profusely on the grass-green, almost wirey shoots. The sharply lobed deciduous leaves are oval and taper to a point. **Growing Conditions:** *K. japonica* does not need any particular consideration as far as soil and sun are concerned, but it rewards a bright location and sufficiently moist, nutrient-containing soil with profuse blossoms. **Varieties:** The best known of the garden varieties is "Pleniflora," which produces double blossoms. In contrast to the original form, it is distinguished by a more vigorous growth and fewer runners. **Recommendations:** Both *K. japonica* and *K. japonica* "Pleniflora" are pollution-resistant and thrive well in an urban environment. This unassuming flowering bush can be easily planted in front of larger woody plants, as part of a border of mixed shrubs, as a solitary specimen in flower beds, or in large tubs. However, it is best if it is not the center of attraction when planted in a tub.

Kolkwitzia amabilis Beautybush

Height: 8′–10′   Diameter: 8′–10′   Soil: 1–2   V–VI   ❊

Origin: *Kolkwitzia* is indigenous to Western China. **Characteristics:** This extremely ornamental flowering bush is distinguished by its particularly elegant shape that features loosely overhanging clusters of blossoms. These appear in profusion in May and June; the individual blossoms are pale pink and funnel-shaped with a yellowish calyx. The deciduous leaves are broadly ovate at their base, taper off, and end in a point. This woody plant is winter-hardy and well suited for an urban environment. Moreover, it greatly resembles *Weigela* except that it is lovelier and more elegant. **Growing Conditions:** *K. amabilis* can thrive satisfactorily in rather poor, dry soil, and it can also manage in partial shade. There is no doubt, however, that a good, deep garden soil rich in nutrients in a protected, sunny location contributes greatly to its optimal development. **Recommendations:** The Beautybush ranks highest on our list of suggested flowering shrubs. Accordingly, whenever possible, it should be featured as the center of attraction. This woody plant also makes an excellent solitary specimen. Given enough space, *K. amabilis* can fully unfold its elegant shape. Its use as a uniform, loosely arranged blooming hedge is also highly recommended. When part of a group, its best neighbors would be graceful shrubs such as *Deutzia* or *Lonicera morrowii.*

Laburnum x watereri   Waterer Laburnum

Height: 26′–32′   Diameter: 13′–16′   Soil: 1–2   V   ❋   !!!

Origin: *Laburnum x watereri* was cultivated by crossing *L. alpinum* with *L. anagyroides*. **Characteristics:** *L. x watereri* grows into large treelike shrubs or smaller to medium-sized trees whose branches and shoots are covered with green bark. It is distinguished by its vigorous growth. The profuse clusters of golden yellow blossoms appear in May and can attain a length of up to 20″. The deciduous leaves are stalked and trifoliate. The individual leaflets are 1¼″–3¼″ long and have an elliptical shape. Despite the beauty of its flowers, *L. x watereri*, like the other species of *Laburnum,* has the disadvantage of being poisonous in all its parts, including the seed pods, which remain hanging on the tree for a long time. **Growing Conditions:** *L. x watereri* does not make any special claims as far as its location in the garden is concerned. It develops to its optimal potential, however, if it is planted in a spot with full sunlight and warm, not too moist, well-drained soil rich in nutrients. Waterer Laburnum also thrives in sandy, somewhat dry soil, but in this case it remains rather small. **Varieties and Species:** Practically the only variety of *L. x watereri* available is "Vossii," which is why it has become so important in horticultural use. *L. alpinum,* Scotch Laburnum, is vigorous in growth and produces small individual blossoms in clusters about 12″ long. *L. anagyroides,* known as Golden Chain, has shorter flower clusters which appear earlier. All varieties and species of *Laburnum* are pollution-resistant and winter-hardy. **Recommendations:** *L. x watereri* is well suited as a solitary specimen on lawns or on similar open surfaces, but it also combines well with other plants such as the smaller conifers. In any case, its high toxicity must be kept in mind and thus it should be planted out of the reach of children.

Ligustrum vulgare   Common Privet

Height: up to 16′   Diameter: 10′   Soil: 1–2   VI–VII   !!!

Origin: *L. vulgare* is indigenous to Europe, North Africa, and Asia Minor. **Characteristics:** The deciduous, elongated oval leaves are smooth, gray-green, and 1¼″–2″ long. The white blossoms appear in the form of panicles in June and July, but only on untrimmed shrubs. They are followed by shiny black berrylike fruits that can grow as large as peas and are poisonous. **Growing Conditions:** The Common Privet is distinguished by its adaptability as far as location is concerned. It can tolerate poor soil and partial shade. **Varieties and Species:** The best known form is "Atrovirens," which is semi-evergreen and whose leaves have a bronze color. "Lodense" is a low evergreen shrub that is brownish green in color. The somewhat hardier *L. ovalifolium* is not completely winter-hardy, but it does have the ability to regenerate after frost damage. **Recommendations:** Predominantly used as a hedge plant; it should be untrimmed for extensive plantings.

Lonicera pileata   Privet Honeysuckle

Origin: *L. pileata* is indigenous to Central and Western China. **Characteristics:** The honeysuckle is a low, flat shrub with outstretched branches and evergreen foliage. The opposite leaves are elongated and oval, and have a shiny deep green color. The bright yellow blossoms, ¼"–½" in size, bloom in May, and out of them develop the small, round violet fruits. This woody plant is pollution-resistant and winter-hardy to a certain extent. **Growing Conditions:** The Privet Honeysuckle makes no particular demands and can thrive even in partial shade. **Varieties:** "Yunnanensis" with its rather vigorous growth is well known, but it does not bloom nor does it bear fruit. **Recommendations:** Because of its dense habit and its evergreen foliage, honeysuckle is well suited as a ground cover and occasionally also as a low hedge. Because of its toxicity, however, it should not be planted where it might be accessible to children.

Lonicera tatarica   Tatarian Honeysuckle

Origin: *L. tatarica* is indigenous to southern Russia, Altei, and Turkestan. **Characteristics:** This versatile and highly recommended woody plant is 10'–13' tall and puts out shoots very early in spring. In open spaces it grows into dense, wide shrubs. The ovate leaves are dark green, 1¼"–2" long, and remain on the bush until deep into the fall. The pale pink blossoms come in pairs about ¾" in diameter. They develop into small, shiny red berrylike fruits. This woody plant is poisonous. **Growing Conditions:** One of the distinguishing features of *L. tatarica* is its adaptability. **Varieties and Species:** The deciduous "Zabelii" is well known; it is a shrub approximately 6' high and produces blossoms ½" long, either white with pink or just pink. Of the evergreens, *L. nitida* and *L. pileata* are recommended. *L. nitida* reaches a height of 6½', produces creamy white blossoms in May and June and develops violet fruits. The winter-hardy *L. pileata* is a flat-growing shrub about 20" tall. Its small white blossoms appear in April and May and have a pleasant fragrance, while the fruits are reddish violet and translucent. *L. ledebourii, L. maackii,* and *L. xylosteum* are semievergreen species. *L. ledebourii* is a shrub 5' tall with dense, dark green leaves; its yellow-orange to reddish-orange blossoms bloom in May and June, and its purplish-black fruits have red cover leaves. *L. maackii* can attain a height of 13'. This plant blooms white in June with its blossoms turning yellowish later on; the fruits are dark red. *L. xylosteum* is 10' tall and produces yellowish-white blossoms in May. **Recommendations:** Because of its adaptability, there is a broad spectrum of uses for the Tatarian Honeysuckle. It can serve as a cover shrub in front of larger woody plants, as undergrowth to loosely arranged, large trees, and can also be used for planting in open areas. This poisonous plant should not be anywhere within reach of children.

Magnolia x soulangeana   Saucer Magnolia

Height: 20'–23'   Diámeter: 13'–16'   Soil: 1–3   V

Origin: *M. x soulangeana* was developed from a cross between *M. denudata* and *M. liliflora.* **Characteristics:** *M. x soulangeana* comes in the form of a shrub as well as of a low-trunked tree. The green deciduous leaves are ovate to elliptical and 4"–6" long. Most characteristic of *M. x soulangeana* are its erect, bell-shaped blossoms, about 4" in length, which appear in great numbers and cover the tree in an absolute ocean of blossoms. The blooms are white and, depending upon the variety, more or less pink to purple on the outside. On the whole, the magnolia is one of the most glorious flowering trees available. **Growing Conditions:** Since it is so highly ornamental, *M. x soulangeana* needs a lot of space that should be protected. The soil should be rich in humus and nutrients and amply watered, especially during the spring and summer months. **Varieties and Species:** "Alba Superba" with silvery white blossoms; "Alexandrina," an early bloomer; "Lennei," wide, bell-shaped blossoms that are violet on the outside; "Lennei Alba," pure white; "Nigra," only 10' tall with narrow, bell-like blossoms that are deep purplish red on the outside. *M. denudata* is a shrub with upright branches, obovate leaves, and creamy white blossoms. It can grow to a height of 6½'–13'. *M. kobus* are shrubs and trees up to 33' tall whose white blossoms appear in April and May before the leaves. *M. liliflora* grows into broad shrubs with short ciliated buds and fragrant purple blossoms. *M. liliflora* "Nigra" has narrower, dark purple blossoms and blooms somewhat later. Popular and pretty is also the slowly growing Star Magnolia, *M. stellata,* which produces white, star-shaped blossoms as early as March and April and is therefore frequently threatened by night frosts. By covering them, however, you can counter such ravages. *M. stellata* "Rosea" with pink buds and white blossoms tinged with pink do well in protected locations, weather permitting. **Recommendations:** The larger varieties of *M. x soulangeana* and *M. kobus* are especially well suited as solitary specimens on sufficiently large lawns. Because of its more modest height, *M. x soulangeana* "Nigra" is preferable for smaller to medium-sized home gardens; the other low varieties work well in daintier corners. Moreover, because their cultivation is difficult and protracted, magnolias are expensive plants. When purchasing one, particular attention should be paid to the overall health and intactness of the shoots, and the plant should have a well-packed, moist root ball.

Malus floribunda   Japanese Flowering Crab Apple

Height: 13'–32'   Diameter: 10'–20'   Soil: 1   V   *

Origin: As far as is known, *M. floribunda* is indigenous to Japan. **Characteristics:** This is an extremely ornamental plant in shrub or tree form. It has a densely branched top with deeply overhanging boughs. The deciduous leaves are single-lobed and green. The luxurious profusion of blossoms appears in May; each individual single blossom is outwardly red and inwardly white. These in turn produce the ³⁄₈" wide ornamental crab apples, which are green at first and later turn yellow with red cheeks. They generally remain on the tree until the beginning of November. Since it does retain its fruits and blossoms for a very long time, this tree is highly prized for its ornamental value. **Growing Conditions:** For its optimal development, *M. floribunda* needs an open, sunny location with medium-heavy to light, well-drained, nutrient-containing soil. **Varieties and Species:** "Atrosanguinea" (illustration), which produces red fruits, is very well known and is considered one of the prettiest of the crab apples. Moreover, this variety is winter-hardy and for the most part resistant to pollution and apple scab. On the whole, the crab apple group is very versatile. The following list mentions only those species and their varieties that are particularly ornamental and have proven successful. The *Malus* hybrid called "Almey" can grow to 13', produces deep purplish-red blossoms, has greenish-bronze foliage and orange colored fruits about ⁴⁄₅" in diameter. *M. coronaria* "Charlottae," 20'–26' tall, blooms late but very profusely and reliably, even in more rugged environments; it has blush-pink blossoms and its autumn foliage is a glorious reddish-orange color. "Profusion," another *Malus* hybrid, has pinkish-red blossoms and reddish-brown fruits. *M. sylvestris* (synonym *M. pumila*) "Pendula" can grow up to 18' tall and has widely overhanging branches, brownish-green leaves and blush-pink blossoms. Its yellowish-red fruits are globular and can range up to 2⅓" in size and are pleasant to the taste. "Eleyi," another *Malus* hybrid, grows to about 18' and has long brown leaves and dark pink blooms. The *Malus* hybrid "Nicoline," 16'–20' tall, has dark red foliage, red blossoms and fruits, and is somewhat sensitive. The *Malus* hybrid "Lemoinei," which can reach a height of 16'–20', has bronze-colored leaves, early, red semi-double blossoms, dark purple fruits; it is not suited for rugged environments. "Calocarpa" is only 13' tall, has pinkish-white blossoms and broad, globular fruits with a deep red color. "Wintergold" is also only 13' tall, has small white blossoms on dense, widely branched ornamental boughs, is reliable and produces small yellow fruits. **Recommendations:** Because of the size the Japanese Flowering Crab Apple can attain, it represents an ornamental tree with particular decorative value for larger gardens and parks. For more modest gardens, one can choose from among the smaller species of *Malus* and their varieties. In contrast to the dessert apple trees, the ornamental apple trees need no regular cutting back; an occasional trimming of older specimens is sufficient.

Philadelphus x virginalis
Mock Orange

Height: 6½'–10'   Diameter: 6½'   Soil: 1–2   VI

Origin: Unknown. **Characteristics:** *Philadelphus x virginalis* forms medium-sized, fast-growing shrubs with gray shoots whose ends tend to hang downward. The deciduous foliage is lance-shaped without any particularly distinguishing characteristics. The white blossoms appear in June and give off a very intense fragrance. On the whole, this woody plant is ornamental and hardy. At first glance the genus *Philadelphus* resembles that of *Deutzia*. However, a simple distinguishing characteristic is that the *Deutzia* branches are hollow inside, whereas those of *Philadelphus* are filled with pulp. **Growing Conditions:** The Mock Orange does not need any special attention. It flourishes in just about any type of soil and tolerates both full sunshine as well as shade. Still, there is no doubt that it will develop particularly well in a sunny location with good soil. **Varieties and Species:** "Snowstorm," medium-sized with snow-white double blossoms. "Girandole," only 6½' tall, slow-growing. Even smaller is "Manteau d'Hermin," 3', especially slow-growing and dense. *P. coronarius,* Sweet Mock Orange, is a very well known species of this genus. Depending upon its location, it can grow 10'–16' in height. Its main branches grow stiff and upright with overhanging lateral shoots; its elongated lanceolate leaves can reach a length of 2¾"–3½". The creamy white blossoms appear in May and June, cling together in clusters and give off a sweet fragrance. Because of its size and shape, *P. coronarius* is recommended as a very attractive flowering tree for solitary or group positioning. *P. inodorus* is also hardy and vigorous and grows to a height of 16'. This equally resistant and adaptable tree blooms in June with fragrant white single blossoms. *P. x lemoinei* is a short and squat ornamental shrub that reaches a height of 4'–5'. It has delicate twigs and small white single blossoms. This particularly hardy and pollution-resistant species makes a very good flowering hedge. **Recommendations:** Mock Oranges remain relatively small and some varieties are not terribly vigorous. This woody plant is therefore especially good for smaller to medium-sized gardens. In addition, it can also be integrated naturally into larger landscapes of bushes and shrubs. With advancing age all varieties and species of *Philadelphus* tend to produce fewer and fewer flowers. This can be mitigated by progressively removing the oldest branches during the winter months.

Picea pungens   Colorado Spruce

Origin: California mountains. **Characteristics:** *P. pungens* is a fast-growing conifer with bald, shiny brownish-orange branches and blue-green needles. **Growing Conditions:** In the course of time *P. pungens* develops into an elegant tree. The Colorado Spruce therefore needs a wide berth with ordinary garden soil that is sufficiently moist but at the same time well drained. Like the other species of *Picea*, *P. pungens* cannot tolerate alkaline soils. **Varieties:** "Glauca" (illustration above) is probably one of the most popular of the conifers. In marked contrast to this popularity is the opinion of many experts that this tree is much too stiff in appearance. But there is no question that the blue-green needles are very ornamental. There are other forms of the "Glauca" variety, for example "Glauca Kosteri." This tree grows to about 32', tapers toward the top and has deep blue-green needles. "Glauca Moerheimii" resembles it, but has longer needles. Well liked are also the following tall species of Picea: *P. abies,* the Norway Spruce, which is the predominant specimen in European conifer forests. Interesting as a weeping variety is "Inversa," which can attain a height of 32'–50' and lets its lower branches rest on the ground. "Acrocona" is expansive, already decked with cones in its early years, and only 16' tall; it is thus well suited for smaller gardens. *P. glauca* (synonym *P. alba*), the White Spruce, grows slowly to a height of 23'. This broad and dense non-sensitive conifer is unfortunately underused. *P. omorica,* the Serbian Spruce, is a slender tree well suited for home gardens. *P. mariana* (synonym *P. nigra*), the Black Spruce, has a wide, irregular shape, is 16' tall and highly frost-resistant. **Recommendations:** *P. pungens* and the other varieties described above are very appropriate for larger gardens and parks. It should be planted in a dominant position as a solitary specimen so that it becomes the center of attraction. Moreover, one should choose the more irregularly shaped specimens and reach less frequently for the stiff, "stepped" varieties.

Picea abies "Nidiformis"   Norway Spruce

Origin: Developed through selection. **Characteristics:** Small pillow-shaped dwarf form without an apical shoot; it is about 3' high. The illustration is representative of many dwarf forms. **Varieties and Species:** The following dwarf forms are recommended: *P. abies* "Echiniformis," only 6½' tall. "Maxwellii," round and flat, about 3' in diameter. "Procumbens," the creeping form that lies flat on the ground and spreads out. "Pygmaea," broad, flat cone-shaped, about 4' tall. "Mariae-Orffiae" with ornamental globose forms. *P. pungens* "Glauca Globosa," globose, 4' tall. "Glauca Procumbens," creeping variety. **Recommendations:** All dwarf forms blend very well into home gardens of just about every description.

Pinus nigra   Austrian Pine

Height: 82'–100'   Diameter: 13'–16'   Soil: 1–2   *   E

Origin: Europe, the Balkans. **Characteristics:** *P. nigra* (sometimes called *P. austriaca*) is a well-known conifer. **Growing Conditions:** Requirements include a very sunny location. *P. nigra* is also satisfied with a somewhat drier, sandy, or stony soil. **Variety:** "Pygmaea" grows only 6½'–10' tall, is dense, and has dark green needles that brighten up a bit in winter. **Recommendations:** The Austrian Pines are used almost exclusively in somewhat poorer soils in forestry as well as in garden and landscape arrangements.

Pinus strobus   Eastern White Pine

Height: 65'–100'   Diameter: 16'–26'   Soil: 1   *   E

Origin: Eastern North America. **Characteristics:** In its natural habitat *P. strobus* can attain a height of 130'–165'. The needles are about 4" long, blue-green, thin and soft. This tree grows rapidly and is winter-hardy. **Growing Conditions:** Because of its size, the Eastern White Pine needs an open, sunny location with deep, sufficiently moist soil. **Variety:** The small variety "Nana" is sometimes sold under the name "Radiata" (illustration upper left).

Pinus mugo   Mugho Pine

Height: 3'–13'   Diameter: 10'–13'   Soil: 2   *   E

Origin: The mountains of Central and Southern Europe. **Characteristics:** In its natural environment the Mugho Pine grows in the form of a creeping shrub with end shoots that reach straight upward. This species should be planted in lower altitudes so that it will be free from the pressure of snow, and the terminal buds ought to be broken open in spring. **Growing Conditions:** A sunny location with a rather poor soil. **Varieties and Species:** "Gnom," flat and round, 5' tall. "Mughus," squat, 10' tall. "Hesse," compact and low, 3'. "Pumilio," low, 3' tall, but several times that in width. **Recommendations:** The low-growing varieties are extremely versatile.

Pinus pumila

Height: 3'–5'   Diameter: 3'–6½'   Soil: 2   E

Origin: Eastern Asia. **Characteristics:** *P. pumila,* sometimes called the Creeping Pine, has a creeping, shrublike appearance and is winter-hardy. **Growing Conditions:** A bright location with well-drained soil. **Varieties and Species:** "Compacta," squat in appearance (illustration lower right). *P. cemba* "Pygmaea," the dwarf form of the Swiss Stone Pine. *P. densiflora* "Pumila," 6½'–10' tall, the globose variety of the Japanese Red Pine. **Recommendations:** *P. pumila* works well in rock gardens.

Potentilla fruticosa   Bush Cinquefoil

Height: 3'–5'   Diameter: 3'   Soil: 1–2   V–IX

Origin: *P. fruticosa* is distributed just about throughout the Northern Hemisphere. **Characteristics:** *P. fruticosa* forms small, 3'–5'-tall shrubs whose main branches grow rigidly upright but whose lateral shoots hang over to a greater or lesser degree depending upon the variety. The deciduous, 3–5 fingered green leaves are ⅜"–1⅛" long. The period of full bloom lies between May and August, but it can extend into September depending upon location, variety, and weather conditions. *P. fruticosa* blooms very profusely with yellow blossoms. It is a hardy, pollution-resistant, small woody plant which can tolerate occasional dry spells and is, on the whole, highly recommended. **Growing Conditions:** This ornamental plant can grow in poor soil, but in every case it needs full sunlight. **Varieties and Species:** The smaller varieties include ''Arbuscula,'' almost a creeping form with blue-green foliage. ''Golden Carpet,'' smaller than ''Arbuscula.'' ''Hachmann's Giant,'' with large, deep golden yellow blossoms. ''Longacre,'' broad and pillow-shaped. ''Pyrenaica,'' smaller still than the above-mentioned plants. ''Farreri,'' particularly attractive with small leaves, 5' tall. ''Goldfinger'' with long-lasting blooms. ''Jackman,'' relatively vigorous. ''Klondike,'' somewhat smaller. ''Sandvedana,'' vigorous growth and white blossoms. ''Tangerine,'' yellow to orange blossoms. *P. fruticosa var. mandschurica* develops into low shrubs with silky, ciliated leaves and white blossoms. **Recommendations:** Keeping the growth characteristics and various colors in mind, the varieties described above can be used in many ways in all kinds of gardens. The vigorously growing varieties are also well suited for flowering hedges.

Pyracantha coccinea   Scarlet Firethorn

Height: 6½'–10'   Diameter: 5'–6½'   Soil: 1–2   V–VI   ❊

Origin: Native to Italy and western Asia. **Characteristics:** Squarrose shrub with thorny shoots and varying degree of density according to the variety. White blossoms appear in May and June in corymb panicles on the previous year's growth. These are followed by an abundance of yellow and reddish-orange fruits. **Growing Conditions:** The Scarlet Firethorn needs good soil in a sunny location, and if necessary can grow in somewhat sandy soil. **Varieties and Species:** ''Praecox,'' dense, wide and squat, 5' tall. ''Bad Zwischenhahn,'' 6½'–10' tall, robust and rich in fruit. ''Golden Charmer,'' 6'–10' tall, yellow fruit. ''Kasan,'' very vigorous in growth with shiny red fruit. ''Orange Charmer,'' graceful, rigidly upright, abundant fruit. ''Orange Glow,'' rigidly upright, 10' tall, and a good fruit-producer. *P. rogersiana* ''Soleil d'Or,'' 6½', yellow fruit. **Recommendations:** Keeping the growth characteristics and the various colors of the fruits in mind, the different varieties of *Pyracantha* can be used in many ways. They are very attractive when planted in front of light-colored house walls, are well suited for covering any surfaces, and can also be used as a tub plant.

Prunus cerasifera Myrobalan Plum

Height: 16'–23'   Diameter: 10'–16'   Soil: 1–5   III–IV   *

Origin: Balkans, Crimea, southwest Siberia, Caucasus, and the Transcaucasus. **Characteristics:** *P. cerasifera* (synonym *P. pissardii*) usually grows into large upright shrubs or trees with a roundish outline. The reddish-brown foliage supplements the ornamental value of the individual pale pink single blossoms. Plumlike edible reddish fruits are occasionally produced. **Growing Conditions:** *P. cerasifera* needs a sunny location and heavy to medium-heavy alkaline soil that is well drained. **Varieties and Species:** Well known is the variety "Nigra," which is distinguished by its darker foliage. *P. mahaleb,* the Mahaleb Cherry, is very attractive in garden settings and needs no particular individual attention. This woody plant is sold in tree or shrub form, has a broad outline and can grow as tall as 16'–33'. The pleasantly fragrant white blossoms appear in May, and the small fruits are black. *P. padus,* the European Bird Cherry, develops into trees or shrubs of 33'–50' in height and a considerable width. The profuse bloom is white and appears in the form of numerous small blossoms that are arranged in hanging clusters. These are followed by black fruits about 3/16" across. This woody plant makes few demands as far as soil is concerned and can tolerate both full sun as well as partial shade. **Recommendations:** *P. cerasifera* is appropriate for smaller to medium-sized gardens and does well, for example, in combinations with yellow blooming forsythias.

Prunus laurocerasus Cherry Laurel

Height: 6½'–13'   Diameter: 5'–10'   Soil: 3–1   V–VI   E

Origin: Balkans, Western Asia, Southern and Western Europe. **Characteristics:** *P. laurocerasus* is an evergreen shrub that grows dense and wide and has leathery elliptical leaves about 4" in length. The profuse white blossoms take on the form of upright candle-shaped clusters. **Growing Conditions:** The Cherry Laurel needs heavy to medium-heavy well-drained soil in full sun, but it can also tolerate partial shade. **Varieties:** "Otto Luyken," broad and very dense, about 3' tall. "Schipkaensis Macrophylla," a little more upright in habit, 6½'–10' tall. "Zabeliana," pronouncedly flat but in the course of time it can reach a height of 6½' or more. **Species:** Of the many attractive species and varieties of *Prunus,* two particular types deserve special mention: *P. incisa* "Moerheimii" blooms very early with white blossoms, is very hardy, and grows in a sideward expansion. *P. sargentii* can attain a height of 50', has pink single blossoms in April, reddish new growth, and a pretty autumn coloration that ranges from orange to carmine red. In later years the original steep outline becomes more rounded. It is reasonably tolerant as far as location is concerned. **Recommendations:** *P. laurocerasus* is a versatile species that can be used as an evergreen plant either as the focus of attention among ground covers, as an interruption among rhododendron, or as a tub plant. It can tolerate shade, so can also be used in northern exposures.

Prunus triloba   Flowering Almond

Height: 6½'   Diameter: 3'   Soil: 1   IV

Origin: China. **Characteristics:** *P. triloba* comes either in the form of a small shrub or little tree. In either case this woody plant has a dense outline with upright, outswept branches. The thick, flat, pink double blossoms bloom in profusion on the previous year's growth. For this reason the Flowering Almond has to be sharply cut back after the bloom. In order to avoid the scrub-brush appearance a radical pruning would give, you should concentrate on trimming only the most vigorous branches. Of course, this does reduce the following year's bloom. Experience has taught that those plants that are propagated from roots are less sensitive to certain diseases than are the grafted varieties. **Growing Conditions:** The Flowering Almond needs a medium-heavy well-drained alkaline soil, but it also thrives in lighter, sandy soil and in any case likes a sunny location. **Species and Varieties:** *P. serrulata,* the Oriental Cherry, comes in numerous varieties. "Amanogawa," 13' tall, rigidly columnar with pale pink blossoms. "Fugenzo," 16' in height, broad at the top with brown shoots and pink, semi-double blossoms. "Kiku-shidare-sakura," 13', a hanging form with pink double blossoms. "Shimidsu Sakura," 14' tall, broad, with snowy white blossoms. "Shirofugen," 30' tall, broad with whitish-pink double blossoms. "Tai Haku," 26' in height, tall with white blooms. *P. subhirtella* is a delicately branched shrub with long-lasting blossoms that grows to about 16' tall. On the whole, this species is recommended. The variety "Accolade" remains somewhat smaller and blooms in April with single to semi-double pink blossoms. "Plena" produces double blossoms. **Recommendations:** *P. triloba* is a popular spring bloomer with many uses. It can be combined especially well in home gardens with harmoniously colored flowering plants of the bulb or shrub description. Moreover, *P. triloba* can be forced from January onward, which means it can be brought to bloom early in heated rooms.

Rhododendron
Kurume and Vuykiana Hybrid Azaleas

Height: 3'   Diameter: 1½'–2'   Soil: 4   IV–VI   E

Origin: This group of Japanese azaleas are indigenous to Japan, as their name suggests, but in some cases it is not always possible to trace their cultivation. **Characteristics:** Similar to other related forms, the Japanese azaleas are categorized together under the genus name of *Rhododendron.* The characteristics of this group include their dwarfed size and their ability to retain their foliage in protected locations until the end of winter. The bloom is profuse and appears in delicate, iridescent colors. A light winter protection against sun and wind is recommended. **Growing Conditions:** Japanese azaleas are sensitive to the ravages of violent storms. This is why these plants prefer a protected location, partial shade, and a well-watered somewhat acidic humus soil. **Varieties:** Recommended are "Beethoven," purple, full bloom in May and June; "Blaauw's Pink," salmon red, May and June; "Favorite," iridescent ruby red, May; "Jeanette," pink with reddish-brown markings, May and June; "Mother's Day," red, April and May; "Orange Beauty," salmon red, tinged with scarlet, April and May; "Schubert," iridescent pink, May and June; "Vuyk's Rosyred," pinkish-red, May and June; "Vuyk's Scarlet," iridescent red, May and June. The following are noted for their small size and small blossoms: "Amoena," violet red, May and June; "Christmas Cheer," pink, May and June; "Esmeralda," pink, May and June; "Hatsugiri," purple, May; "Hinomayo," pink, May; "Hinodegiri," dark ruby red, May; "Little Beauty," ruby red, May.

Rhododendron   Williams Rhododendron

Height: 2½'–5'   Diameter: 1½'–3'   Soil: 4   IV–V

Origin: The available varieties have been developed via cultivars. In the following description, special mention is made of those cultivars of the German horticulturist Hobbie in Linswege. **Characteristics:** Williams Rhododendron hybrids are densely growing, large-blossomed plants with round to oval foliage that can be brought to bloom even in somewhat alkaline soils if treated with a sufficient addition of humus. **Growing Conditions:** Like other species of *Rhododendron,* the Williams hybrids prefer partially shady spots with moist, slightly acidic humus soil. But, as already mentioned, they can also tolerate some lime. **Varieties:** The following plants are recommended: "Oldenburg," pink, bell-shaped blossoms on dense, globose bushes, on the whole robust, grows to about 5' in height; "Wega," bright pink, similar to "Oldenburg" but looser in shape, reaches a height of 5'; "Bremen," carmine red, flat globose shape, somewhat more demanding as far as climate and location are concerned, only 30" tall; "Garden Director Glocker," bright pink, thick and bushy, 4' tall. **Recommendations:** All of these smaller forms of *Rhododendron* can be used in a variety of ways in gardens of all descriptions.

Rhododendron   Catawba hybrids

Height: 6½'–26'   Diameter: 6½'–16'   Soil: 4   V–VI   E

Origin: Developed via horticultural cultivation, frequently involving *R. catawbiense.* **Characteristics:** Under optimal conditions these evergreen bushes can attain a height of up to 26'. In more rugged regions they only grow to between 6½' to 10' tall. As a rule, the lilac-colored varieties are hardier than the others. **Growing Conditions:** *Rhododendron* hybrids need protected, partially shady locations with sufficiently moist, somewhat acidic soils rich in humus. The higher the humidity the better, and the water should be free of lime. **Varieties:** "Catawbiense Grandiflorum," violet, broadly globuse, dull green foliage and a late bloomer (June); "Everestianum," bright purplish violet, squat, broad shape, full bloom early in June; "Humboldt," bright purplish violet with dark red spots, broad compact shape with large, dark green foliage, early bloomer (beginning of May); "Cunningham's White," white with pale purple overtones, hardy, dense with dark green foliage and an early bloom (May); "Jacksonii," white to blush-pink, small, dense and globose, early bloom (beginning of May); "Catharina van Tol," pink, squat shape, dull green leaves, late bloom (beginning of June); "Nova Zembia," iridescent red, medium growth, very hardy; "America," ruby red, loose shape, very hardy; "Roseum Elegans," ruby red, broad, squat shape, thick foliage, late bloom (beginning of June); "Dr. H. C. Dresselhuys," dark ruby red, large with a shape that is taller than it is broad, large leaves, early bloom (May) and hardy; "Caracteus," purplish red, upright, taller than wide, late bloom (beginning of June).

Rhododendron   Knap Hill and Exbury Hybrid Azaleas

Height: 5'–6½'   Diameter: 5'   Soil: 4   V–VI

Origin: Great Britain, hence the common name "English Azaleas." **Characteristics:** These very pretty varieties are distinguished by large blossoms with brilliant colors. The introduction of this group has completely changed and greatly enriched the available selection of *Rhododendron.* **Growing Conditions:** See above under *Rhododendron* hybrids. **Varieties and Species:** The following May and June bloomers have proven to be particularly popular choices from among the rich selection of varieties: "Berryrose," pink with yellow spots; "Cecile," pale pink with yellow spots; "Gibraltar," copper red; "Golden Eagle," yellowish bronze; "Golden Sunset," golden yellow with brown spots; "Klondyke," yellowish bronze; "Persil," pure white; "Pink Delight," pink with yellow spots; "Royal Command," copper red; "Stan," scarlet. **Recommendations:** True for all *Rhododendrons* is the fact that they can be used as the focus of attention in any landscape. In larger numbers they are very attractive as undergrowth among loosely distributed large trees.

Rhus typhina Staghorn Sumac

Height: 10'–16'   Diameter: 6½'–13'   Soil: 1–3   VI–VII   ❋

Origin: *R. typhina* is indigenous to the eastern regions of North America.
Characteristics: This woody plant usually grows in the form of a short-trunked, characteristically branched tree or shrub; two new shoots develop on every branching point. This gives the Staghorn Sumac its squarrose shape and, with increasing age, its umbrellalike top. The young shoots are thick and hairy. *R. typhina* is dioecious with male and female plants. The alternate compound deciduous leaves have elongated, lance-shaped individual leaflets up to 31 in number and up to 12" in length. These leaves range in color from yellow to orange and purplish red in the fall. The bloom appears in June and July in the form of upright, terminal, and spiked blossoms. The female plants produce purplish-red ornamental fruits which remain on the tree until winter. On the whole *R. typhina,* particularly the female plant, is a very decorative specimen whose only disadvantage is its production of runners. **Growing Conditions:** *R. typhina* likes light soil with an ample supply of moisture but without standing water. In addition, a location with full sunlight is recommended. **Varieties and Species:** The Staghorn Sumac has one highly recommended variety, "Dissecta." The irregular, pinnately dissected leaves are 12" long and have deeply cut leaflets. These, too, turn from yellow to orange to purplish red in the fall. *R. typhina* has many related species, of which the most interesting is *R. glabra* because of its similar characteristics and its resistance to frost. This woody plant generally grows more slowly than *R. typhina* and not as tall. The pinnate leaves are between 6" and 8" long and are likewise lance-shaped and pointed. In addition to its striking appearance, this specimen, too, has the advantage of an especially attractive autumn coloration. The female plants are distinguished by their pinkish-brown fruits. *R. glabra* has an even stronger tendency than *R. typhina* to produce runners, but in spite of this, it is appropriate for the same uses. **Recommendations:** Because of its size, *R. typhina* is well suited for smaller gardens and is an excellent choice for a solitary specimen in home gardens or front yards, near terraces, or in atrium gardens, and it can also be planted in large tubs. Several specimens can be grouped together on lawns. Since this woody plant is pollution-resistant and hardy, it is also appropriate for planting in inner city parks. In any case one must remember its tendency to produce runners, but this can also be used to advantage in that they can be carefully removed and presented to other gardeners as welcome gifts.

Ribes sanguineum   Winter Currant

Height: 6½'–10'   Diameter: 5'–8'   Soil: 1   IV–V   ✻

Origin: *R. sanguineum* is indigenous to North America. **Characteristics:** These plants set their shoots early in spring, are of medium growth, and in later years have to be trimmed. The deciduous foliage has 3 to 5 lobes and is dark green. The red blossom clusters appear in April or May, depending upon the location. Generally speaking, a very worthwhile shrub. **Growing Conditions:** *R. sanguineum* likes sunny to partially shady locations with nutrient-containing soil and no standing water. **Varieties:** "Atrorubens" with deep dark red blossoms, in rugged areas frequently susceptible to freeze-back. "King Edward VII," deep red, large clusters of blossoms, good growth. "Pulborough Scarlet," deep red blossoms with white centers, very good growth. **Recommendations:** *R. sanguineum* and its related varieties are exceptionally well suited for combination with *Forsythia* and, like that plant, can be used for many purposes.

Robinia pseudacacia   Black Locust

Height: 50'–82'   Diameter: 26'–50'   Soil: 1–2   VI   ✻   !!!

Origin: Central United States. **Characteristics:** This late-blooming woody plant can develop into a shrub or tree. It displays a loose and open shape. While the older branches have a deeply gutted bark, the younger shoots are covered with thorns. The deciduous leaves are alternately pennate, and the individual leaflets are elongated, oval, and about 1¼"–1½" long. In June, *R. pseudacacia* produces luxuriantly fragrant white blossoms in pendulous clusters. These are followed by brown leguminous fruits. **Variety:** "Umbraculifera" is globose in shape and requires a regular trimming. **Growing Conditions:** The Black Locust will grow in almost any soil, even poor sandy soils and wasteland. It likes full sun. **Recommendations:** Because of its adaptability, *R. pseudacacia* can be used for many purposes; as a rounded form to assure privacy from passersby or as a freely growing shrub in larger gardens and parks. Its tendency to produce runners helps retain the soil, especially helpful when it is planted on slopes. Moreover, flowering *Robinias* are an excellent addition to any bee and butterfly garden.

Robinia hispida   Rose Acacia

Height: 5'–6½'   Soil: 1–2   VI–IX

Origin: North America. **Characteristics:** The Rose Acacia is a shrubby plant, 6½' tall with relatively brittle shoots and pennate leaves. The papilionaceous blossoms appear in short clusters. **Growing Conditions:** *R. hispida* needs a sunny, protected location. **Variety:** "Macrophylla" with pinkish-red blossoms. **Recommendations:** This shrub can grow as a solitary specimen in front of larger woody plants or among summer flowers.

Rosa centifolia   Cabbage Rose

Height: 6½'–10'   Diameter: 5'–6½'   Soil: 1   VI–VIII   ✱

Origin: The origin of *R. centifolia* is unclear, but it is probably indigenous to the Caucasus. **Characteristics:** A large bush with bright green overhanging branches. The blossoms resemble tea cups; they are double, very fragrant, and range from white to red. The stems and sepals are covered with bristles. **Growing Conditions:** Like all roses, *R. centifolia,* likes a well-drained well watered soil rich in nutrients and a lot of sunshine. **Varieties:** Particularly attractive is "Paul Ricoult" (illustration above), but equally recommended are "Muscosa" and "Constance Spry." "Muscosa" is a densely branched variety that is also known as Moss Rose. **Recommendations:** *R. centifolia* is an "old fashioned" variety and thus fits well in gardens of this description. Moreover, cabbage roses combine very well with wild roses and blend in well among loosely arranged, tall groups of woody plants.

Rosa foetida   Austrian Brier Rose

Height: 8'   Diameter: 6½'–8'   Soil: 1   V–VI

Origin: Western and Southern Asia. **Characteristics:** A sizable bush with brown overhanging branches whose green leaves fall relatively early. The blossoms appear in May and June and consist of single flowers with a diameter of 2"–2¾", arranged individually or in groups. *R. foetida* was one of the parent plants in the crossbreeding of yellow and orange cultivars. The yellow flowers of the Austrian Brier Rose have a somewhat unpleasant scent. **Variety:** "Capucine Bicolore" (illustration lower left). **Growing Conditions:** A sunny location with a well-drained, moist soil rich in nutrients. **Recommendations:** Similar to those for *R. centifolia.*

Rosa rugosa   Rugosa Rose

Height: 5'   Diameter: 2½'–3'   V–IX   ✱

Origin: Korea, Japan, Northern China. **Characteristics:** Upright bush with very thorny shoots and a strong tendency to produce runners. The luxuriant deciduous foliage is deep green and turns yellow in the fall. The single pink to red blossoms, about 3" wide, are followed by roundish flat, large, orange to red edible fruits. **Growing Conditions:** This bush thrives in full sunshine even in the poorest of sandy soils, but it does not like acidic or alkaline soils. **Species:** Of all the "Wild Roses," the following species are especially noteworthy: *R. canina,* the Dog Rose, is 6½'–10' tall, produces single pink blossoms and rosehips. *R. multiflora* 6½'–10' tall, has pendulous branches and blooms in June and July with single white blossoms; it also produces numerous red fruits. *R. nitida* is 20"–30" tall, blooms in June or July with single pink flowers and produces long-lasting fruits. **Recommendations:** *R. rugosa* is suitable for flowering hedges and for adding green coloring to sun-drenched embankments.

Rosa   Polyantha hybrids

Height: 1½'–5'   Diameter: 1'–3'   Soil: 1   VI–X

Origin: Not completely traceable. **Characteristics:** Unlike the hybrid tea roses that produce one blossom per stem, the stems of the *Polyantha* hybrids bear corymb-shaped flower clusters. As a result of intensive cultivation, these hybrid forms have larger individual flowers and a greater profusion of blooms, even though they originally stem from *Polyantha* roses bearing only small blossoms. The color of the flowers has also become more brilliant. Roses with particularly large individual flowers resembling tea roses are called *Floribunda* hybrids. A longer blooming season in the case of the *Floribunda* can be increased by gently cutting back after the first bloom and by continually removing the wilted corymbs throughout the summer. **Growing Conditions:** The *Polyantha* hybrids need a strong, deep, moist, and nutrient-containing soil in a sunny spot free of standing water. In somewhat more rugged environments they can be protected for the winter by surrounding and covering them with fir branches. **Varieties:** "Sarabanda" (illustration above) is preferred among a number of varieties. **Recommendations:** The above-mentioned group of hybrids is well suited for both smaller and larger rose beds, and the best advice would be to choose the variety whose color fits in best with the surroundings. *Polyantha* roses can be combined with conifers, wild shrubs, grasses, or blue-blooming wildflowers like *Salvia farinacea* or *S. nemorosa,* as long as the roses themselves dominate the scene.

Rosa   Long-stemmed Roses

Height: 1½'–6½'   Diameter: 1½'–3'   Soil: 1   VI–X

Origin: Long-stemmed roses are a special sub-stock of cultivated tea hybrids, *Polyantha* hybrids, or rambling roses. **Characteristics:** The grafting position for stem roses is at the base of the crown—that is, above ground. This explains the greater danger to these plants of frost and wind damage. One preventive measure is a stable support trellis; another is that, after cutting back the shoots, the remaining stump should be packed with hay as a protection against drying winter winds and sun.

Rosa   Hybrid Tea Roses

Height: 1½'–5'   Diameter: 16"–2½'   Soil: 1   VI–X

Origin: Not precisely known. **Characteristics:** These specially cultivated flowers have a pleasant fragrance and appear individually on the current year's growth. **Growing Conditions:** The same as for *Polyantha* roses. **Varieties:** A great number of varieties are available, and particularly attractive is the "Superstar" (illustration lower right). **Recommendations:** These plants make excellent individual specimens for collectors and, in the right color combination, are also well suited for inclusion in rose gardens.

Rosa Climbing Roses

Height: 5'–16'   Width: 13'–20'   Soil: 1   VI–VII, IX–X

Origin: No longer fully traceable. **Characteristics:** Climbing roses (illustration above) are not considered members of the climbing plants because they neither climb nor wind. They are actually spreaders that "climb" up other woody plants with the help of their long shoots, or canes, which are covered with thorns. This is why they have to be provided with support structures in the form of espaliers, pergolas, etc., to which the young shoots can attach themselves. Fences and walls can also serve in this capacity. **Growing Conditions:** Climbing roses like a sunny location and a strong, deep, moist soil rich in nutrients but without standing water. While young and in more rugged environments, these plants are sensitive to frost. As a protection against this, several suggestions have proven successful; these include tying them down, or surrounding or covering them with fir branches. These roses become hardier in their later years. To trim these plants, the older branches should be removed together with the weak shoots in order to encourage the more vigorous of the previous year's growth. **Varieties:** The following varieties are only some of the available types: "American Pillar," pink single blossoms with a white center; "Flame Dance," blood red, double blossoms; "Park Director Riggers" (illustration lower left), red blossoms throughout the summer and on into the fall; "Dortmund," scarlet single flowers with a yellow center, frequent bloomings; "Sympathy," velvety dark red, large double blossoms, frequent bloomings. **Recommendations:** Climbing roses are excellently suited for covering support structures such as espaliers and pergolas. A columnar climbing structure has an elegant effect when combined with rose beds of various harmonious colors.

Rosa sweginzowii

Height: 6½'–8'   Diameter: 6½'–10'   Soil: 1   VI–VII   ❄

Origin: Northwest China. **Characteristics:** *R. sweginzowii* is a typical representative of a group of wild roses that produces truly unusual blossoms but whose main ornamental value lies in its decorative fruit. *R. sweginzowii* grows in relatively large bushes with bright red single blossoms followed by long-lasting large red rosehips (illustration lower right). **Growing Conditions:** Comparable to those of the other roses, but, if necessary, this species can also tolerate a somewhat poorer soil. **Species:** A few other fruit-bearing species are worth mentioning. *R. hugonis* grows to a height of about 6½', and its graceful shoots are densely covered with yellow single flowers that appear as early as May. *R. moyesii* can be as tall as 10', has iridescent scarlet single blossoms and develops long red rosehips. *R. glauca* (synonym *R. rubrifolia*) grows to a height of 10', has reddish-blue leaves, pink blossoms, and very pretty fruit. **Recommendations:** Well suited for wild rose hedges, as a solitary specimen, and in combination with low species of *Juniper, Cotoneaster,* and barberries.

Salix alba White Willow

Height: 50'–80'   Diameter: 30'–50'   Soil: 1–3   IV

Origin: Russia to Eastern Asia. **Characteristics:** *S. alba* is a tall tree with a broad outline whose bark becomes deeply cracked with age. The oval deciduous leaves grow to a length of 2"–4" and are thickly covered with silvery silky hairs on both sides. The catkins that appear in April lack ornamental value. **Growing Conditions:** *S. alba,* like all willows, makes few special demands as far as the soil is concerned, but it does like sufficiently moist, somewhat acidic soil in sunny locations. **Varieties and Species:** "Liempde," particularly rapid growth with widely outstretched tops. "Tristis," the weeping form. "Tristis Resistenta," a weeping form that is resistant against willow diseases. *S. caprea,* the Goat Willow, sometimes called the "French" Pussy Willow, grows in the form of large shrubs or small trees and is a valuable pioneer plant for use on hillsides and slopes. It also grows well in poor situations, such as in front of or below large trees. *S. caprea* "Mas" is a form of a particularly beautifully blooming male Goat Willow. *S. caprea* "Pendula" is a mutation of the male form of Goat Willow with hanging branches. When grafted onto twigs, the shoots can hang down to the ground. Since this tree does not grow very tall, it is often used as a solitary specimen on lawns of home gardens. *S. cinerea* are upright shrubs about 16' tall whose leaves, which later turn a dull green, are initially covered with gray hairs. The catkins are 2"–3" long. *S. daphnoides* comes in tree or shrub form and can attain a height of 20'–26'. Typical of this species are the bluish-white, frosted younger shoots. *S. petiolaris* (synonym *S. gracilis*) is an ornamental shrub suitable for use in low hedges. *S. purpurea,* the Purple Osier, usually grows into 10' shrubs with slender shiny reddish-brown shoots. The typical willow leaves are about 4" long. This woody plant is used predominantly for landscape purposes in virgin and poor soil following construction work. *S. purpurea* "Gracilis" is only 3' tall and works well as a small hedge, and in rock gardens. *S. matsudana* "Tortuosa," the Corkscrew or Contorted Willow, forms pretty but not very tall trees whose younger shoots are twisted like corkscrews. *S. x smithiana* is the result of crossbreeding *S. cinerea* and *S. viminalis* and forms medium-sized shrubs that are marked by an early and profuse display of catkins. **Recommendations:** *Salix alba* and its varieties can be used to great advantage in larger open spaces near bodies of water. "Liempde" also makes a good windscreen.

Sambucus nigra   European Elder

Height: 16′–23′   Diameter: 10′–13′   Soil: 1–2   VI–VII   ❋

Origin: Europe to Western Siberia. **Characteristics:** In many places *S. nigra* is also known by the name of lilac. It is a generally popular, vigorously growing shrub with a light bark. Its shoots are filled with a loose white pulp. The deciduous leaves are composed of five dark green pinnate leaflets, each one elliptical and pointed and between 4″ and 6″ long. The small, cream-white blossoms appear in June and July in the form of large flat corymbs. The blossoms are followed later in the summer and on toward fall by blue-black edible fruits. **Growing Conditions:** *S. nigra* is undemanding, and can get on well even in virgin soil. In good soil the European Elder can develop into a dignified woody plant if given enough room. *S. nigra* tolerates full direct sun as well as shady locations. **Species:** A close relative is *S. racemosa*, the European Red Elder. It is less vigorous in growth (6½′–13′), blooms in April and May, and produces red berrylike fruit. This species, too, tolerates sun and shade to an equal degree and is undemanding. **Recommendations:** The European Elder is a rustic woody plant. For this reason it is predominantly used in rural areas, in villages and in open landscapes. Because of its ability to tolerate shade, *S. nigra* can also be located in front of or under large woody plants. The berries serve as food for birds. Moreover, *S. nigra* can also tolerate salty air, and can thus be planted near the sea.

Skimmia japonica   Japanese Skimmia

Height: 5′   Diameter: 3′   Soil: 1–3   V   ❋   E

Origin: Japan. **Characteristics:** The Japanese Skimmia is a small, globose evergreen plant that is dioecious; there are plants with exclusively male blossoms and plants with exclusively female blossoms. The former are frequently sold under the name *S. fragrans,* while the female plants are called *S. oblata.* The evergreen leaves are dense, elongated and elliptical, reaching a length of 3¼″–4¾″. They are rather leathery to the touch and are a light green on top. In addition to its evergreen foliage, the bright red, flattened, globular berrylike fruits (up to ⅜″ in diameter) are very decorative. **Growing Conditions:** *S. japonica* likes strong, nutrient-containing humus soil. The location should have partial to full shade and, in more rugged regions, should be provided with sufficient protection during the winter months. Experience with other sensitive woody plants suggests some winter protection. **Recommendations:** *S. japonica* can be planted alone or in small groups as the center of attraction among flat ground covers. This woody plant is also itself quite appropriate for use as a ground cover over larger areas. *S. japonica* is very popular for roof and terrace gardens, for planting in tubs, or as undergrowth for medium-sized plants in shady locations.

Sorbus aucuparia European Mountain Ash

Height: 33'–50'   Diameter: 13'–16'   Soil: 1–2   V   *

Origin: *S. aucuparia* is native to Europe, Asia Minor, and Western Siberia. **Characteristics:** *S. aucuparia* usually comes in the form of relatively small trees with loose outlines. The deciduous leaves are pinnate. The bloom is followed in the summer by ornamental shiny red fruits about the size of peas, which, like the blossoms, are arranged in corymb panicles. **Varieties and Species:** "Edulis," beautiful, large outline; "Fastigiata," slow-growing, columnar, with blue-green foliage and deep red fruits that remain on the tree for a long time: "Xanthocarpa," yellow fruits; "Pendula" and "Pendula Variegata," overhanging varieties with yellow foliage. *S. aucuparia var. edulis*, the Moravian Rowan is widely distributed; its edible fruits are particularly large, rich in vitamins and pectin, and can be made into a jam. *S. americana* develops into large shrubs or small trees and makes a very good solitary specimen. *S. aria* is between 26' and 30' tall, conical in shape, and has sharply toothed green leaves that are white and hairy on the underside. *S. intermedia* is indigenous to Scandinavia, where it grows in a squat form to about 30'. The May bloom is followed by relatively large reddish-orange fruits. This species is particularly wind-resistant and can tolerate a city environment and street salt. **Recommendations:** Because of its ornamental fruits, the European Mountain Ash is very versatile. It is suitable for an open landscape as well as a cityscape. It is frequently used along streets, in large gardens and parks, and even in large planters. This tree is hardy and fairly tolerant.

Spiraea x vanhouttei Vanhoutte Spirea

Height: 6½'   Diameter: 5'–6½'   Soil: 1   IV–V

Origin: *S. x vanhouttei* is a cross between *S. cantoniensis* and *S. trilobata*. **Characteristics:** *S. x vanhouttei* is a 6½' shrub with pronounced pendulous lateral branches. The small, oval-rhomboidic leaflets are slightly lobed and toothed. The small white blossoms appear in the form of corymbs and luxuriously decorate the previous years' growth. **Growing Conditions:** *S. x vanhouttei* is an undemanding plant as far as soil is concerned, but it does need a sunny location. **Species and Varieties:** A somewhat more gracefully shaped shrub with narrower leaves is the hybrid *S. x arguta,* which produces white blooms in April and May. A very rewarding small plant is *S. x bumalda.* It grows to a height of about 2½'–3' and blooms on the current year's growth in the form of terminal red corymbs. This species should be cut back to slightly above ground level at the end of winter if it is to bloom with any vigor later on. The popular variety *S. x bumalda* "Anthony Waterer" has carmine red blossoms. "Froebeilii" produces deep purplish-red blossoms. **Recommendations:** *S. x vanhouttei* is well suited both as a solitary specimen and as part of a mixed group or as an open hedge. All of the spireas named above are hardy and can tolerate city air.

Syringa vulgaris   Common Lilac

Height: 10'–16'   Diameter: 6½'–13'   Soil: 1–2   V

Origin: *S. vulgaris* is indigenous to Southeastern Europe and Western Asia.
Characteristics: *S. vulgaris* develops into dense and upright shrubs whose attractive blossoms (illustration above) appear in May on the ends of the previous year's growth. The varieties mentioned below have all been cultivated from *S. vulgaris*. Lilacs tend to produce runners. In removing these runners, it is not enough to cut them off at the ground; rather, they must be dug out in such a way that they are separated from the roots or can be taken out with the roots. The faded blossoms should be removed because they are unattractive and weaken the plant by sapping strength in order to produce seeds. Older specimens can bear radical pruning, but the undergrowth then frequently tends to produce more runners. **Growing Conditions:** Lilacs need a sunny location with deep, nutrient-containing, sandy loamy soil with an ample lime content. **Varieties:** "Ludwig Spaeth," deep purple, single blossoms, particularly popular member of the dark varieties (illustration lower right); "Queen Luise," white single blossoms that bloom even when the plant is older; "Marie Legraye," white single blossoms, popular variety: "Rhum von Horstenstein," lavender, single blossoms, very large, broad panicles; "Charles Joly," deep purple double blossoms; "Mme Lemoine," white double blossoms; "Mme Antoine Buchner," violet double blossoms, late blooming; "Katharina Havemeyer," dark violet double blossoms, rather early bloomer; "Primrose," bright yellow single blossoms. **Recommendations:** Lilacs can be shown to advantage both as solitary specimens in smaller gardens and as members of a group in larger gardens and parks. They also go well with laburnum.

Syringa x swegiflexa   Swegiflexa Lilac

Height: 10'–13'   Diameter: 6½'–10'   VI–VII

Origin: *S. x swegiflexa* was bred by crossing *S. reflexa* with *S. sweginzowii*.
Characteristics: In its overall appearance *S. x swegiflexa* resembles its parent plant *S. reflexa* (Nodding Lilac). Large pink blossoms appear in June and July. While still buds, they display a darker color. On the whole, the bloom is more profuse and remains longer than *S. reflexa's*. **Growing Conditions:** *S. x swegiflexa* likes nutrient-containing, well-drained, slightly alkaline soil in sunny locations (illustration lower left). **Species:** *S. josikaea* is also called the Hungarian Lilac in keeping with its origins. This upright shrub grows to 10'–13' and blooms in June, producing dark bluish-violet blossoms in the form of narrow upright panicles about 8" long. *S. sweginzowii* is also a pretty plant. Unlike the varieties of *S. vulgaris*, *S. x swegiflexa* is much less distributed, not because of its unsuitability, but merely because it is relatively unfamiliar. *S. x swegiflexa* is useful both as a solitary specimen and as part of a group arrangement in home gardens and larger private estates. *S. x swegiflexa* can also be planted in large tubs.

Symphoricarpos albus   Snowberry

Height: 5'–6½'   Soil: 1–2   VI–IX   ❋   !!!

Origin: *Symphoricarpos albus* is indigenous to North America and can be found in the north from Quebec to Alaska and in the south to Virginia, Michigan, and Arizona. **Characteristics:** *S. albus* is also known under the synonymous old name of *S. racemosus.* The Snowberry is a long-lived, dense, runner-producing shrub. Its young shoots have a smooth bark. The oval lance-shaped leaves are deciduous, opposite, and smooth on both sides. There is no particular autumn coloration. The small pink blossoms appear on the terminal or central spikes or in clusters from June to September. They are followed by the typical, round, white berrylike fruit about ⅜" in diameter and filled with a gaseous pulp ("exploding peas"). These usually remain hanging on the bush until winter. On the whole, the Snowberry is considered a robust woody plant. **Growing Conditions:** *S. albus* does not make any great demands concerning its location. This shrub fares well in just about any type of soil, but it rewards good soil with a corresponding optimal development. *S. albus* can certainly tolerate full direct sunlight, but it also thrives in partial or full shade. **Varieties and Species:** The varieties *S. albus var. albus* and *S. albus var. laevigatus* are recommended. One specific variety deserving mention is *S. albus* "Constance Spry," which is distinguished by a dense growth and large white berrylike fruits. *S. x chenaultii* was developed from a cross between *S. microphyllus* and *S. orbiculatus.* The blossoms that appear in June and July are followed by globular reddish fruits. The variety "Hancock" is neither tall (30") nor wide and is therefore suitable as a ground cover for larger areas. *S. orbiculatus* grows to 6½'–10', blooms from July to August, and develops a reddish autumn coloring. The scarlet fruits remain hanging on the bush for a long time. **Recommendations:** Because of its density, *S. albus* is well suited as an untrimmed hedge and for use in an urban setting. Moreover, due to its tolerance for shade, this shrub can also be planted in front of or beneath large shade trees.

Tamarix pentandra   Five Stamen Tamarisk

Height: 10'–16'   Diameter: 10'–13'   Soil: 1–2   VIII–IX

Origin: Southeastern Europe. **Characteristics:** Like the other species of *Tamarix, T. pentandra* has a peculiar appearance. Its characteristics include pendulous branches, tiny, scaly deciduous leaves, and feathery pale pink blossoms. **Growing Conditions:** The tamarisks prefer direct sunlight and a light, warm soil with a moderate amount of lime. **Species:** Worth mentioning are *T. gallica, T. parviflora,* and *T. tetrandra.* **Recommendations:** As with the other species of *Tamarix, T. pentandra* can be planted alone or in groups on open stretches of lawn or near natural stone walls (such as sandstone). All tamarisks work well with conifers.

Taxus cuspidata   Japanese Yew

Height: 6½'   Diameter: 3'–5'   Soil: 1   ✳   !!!

Origin: *T. cuspidata* is indigenous to Japan, Korea, and Manchuria. **Characteristics:** This is a species of *Taxus* that is similar in many respects to *T. baccata* (see below). The distinguishing characteristics include the more pointed bud scales and the thicker needles, also sharply pointed. Like all species of *Taxus, T. cuspidata* grows relatively slowly. With the exception of the red flesh of the fruit, all the remaining parts of the yew are poisonous. Furthermore, the yew is dioecious, that is, divided between male and female plants. **Growing Conditions:** All yews like sufficiently moist, nutrient-containing soil without standing water. They can also tolerate shady locations and some wind. **Variety:** "Nana" produces thick, expansive shrubs up to 6½' in height which are distinguished by their vigorous growth. **Recommendations:** *T. cuspidata* can be displayed as a solitary specimen, as a member of a group, or as a hedge. As in the case of the following species, *T. cuspidata* should not be planted within reach of children because of its toxicity.

Taxus baccata   English Yew

Height: 30'   Diameter: 13'–16'   Soil: 1   ✳   E   !!!

Origin: *T. baccata* is native to Europe as well as to the Caucasus, Asia Minor, Iran, and Northwestern Africa. **Characteristics:** The slowly growing *T. baccata* is also distinguished by a dense growth and can be trimmed to form hedges or specific shapes. **Growing Conditions:** *T. baccata,* too, likes porous soil with a sufficient supply of water and nutrients. **Varieties:** "Fastigiata" grows in upright columns, has relatively large needles and should only be planted in protected places. "Erecta" has smaller needles, does not grow into such a columnar shape, and is better able to withstand the winter. "Erecta Aureovariegata" is a bright yellow, needled variety and is distinguished by its hardiness. "Overeynderei" develops a broad and upright outline and has delicate needles. **Recommendations:** *T. baccata* is predominantly used as a hedge plant.

Taxodium distichum   Common Bald Cypress

Height: 50'–65'   Diameter: 13'–20'   Soil: 3

Origin: North America. **Characteristics:** *T. distichum* grows into sizable trees that are covered with light green, soft upright needles arranged in two rows along the twigs. These needles turn reddish brown in the autumn and fall off in winter. *T. distichum* is densely covered with branches and forms pyramid-shaped outlines. **Growing Conditions:** The Bald Cypress prefers moist but not terribly wet soil near a source of ground water. Excessive water supply can cause knee or air roots. **Recommendations:** Because of their considerable dimensions, these trees are appropriate for extensive grounds.

Thuja orientalis   Oriental Arborvitae

Height: 33'   Diameter: 10'–13'   Soil: 1   E   !!!

Origin: Eastern Asia. **Characteristics:** *T. orientalis* strongly resembles the much more widely distributed *T. occidentalis* and forms pyramid-shaped trees that terminate in bluntly pointed tops. They are densely covered with fan-shaped branches. The light green scaley leaves turn a brownish color in winter. In contrast to *T. occidentalis, T. orientalis* is susceptible to frost in rugged areas and severe winters. **Growing Conditions:** Like all members of this species, *T. orientalis* likes deep, well-drained sandy clay soil with sufficient moisture but no standing water. **Varieties:** An attractive variety is "Bermannii" (illustration above). The variety "Aurea Nana" is well suited for smaller gardens because of its less vigorous growth. Equally desirable for this purpose is "Rosedalis Compacta." **Recommendations:** The original form can be used as solitary specimens or for hedges in climatically favorable areas, while the less vigorously growing forms commend themselves for smaller gardens.

Tsuga canadensis   Canada Hemlock

Height: 50'–65'   Diameter: 20'–26'   Soil: 1   E

Origin: North America. **Characteristics:** With their pendulous lateral branches, the Canada Hemlock can be counted among the graceful evergreen conifers. In the course of time it does grow into a considerable tree whose ultimate dimensions are frequently not taken into consideration at the time of planting. Like the yew, the Canada Hemlock also tolerates shady locations. **Growing Conditions:** *T. canadensis* needs hardy but at the same time porous soil that is well provided with water and fertilizer. **Varieties:** "Bennett" is appropriate for use in small garden plots, because it grows to only about 3' tall and 6½'–10' wide. This variety has a pale green coloring to its needles and remains squat and dense. The tips of the boughs hang over slightly. "Pendula" is a weeping form that is also less vigorous than others and remains wider than it is high. **Recommendations:** *T. canadensis* should be used in its original form only for larger landscaped gardens.

Thuja plicata   Giant Arborvitae

Height: 33'–50'   Diameter: 13'–16'   Soil: 1   E   !!!

Origin: North America. **Characteristics:** Because of its enormous size in its native habitat (up to 190'), *T. plicata* is also known as the gigantic "Tree of Life." In contrast to *T. occidentalis,* its needles, which remain green even in winter, smell like apples. **Growing Conditions:** The growing conditions correspond to those of the other species of *Thuja.* **Varieties:** The columnar "Excelsa" and the hardy "Dura" are very popular. **Recommendations:** Only for larger gardens and landscapes.

Viburnum plicatum   Japanese Snowball

Origin: *V. plicatum* (synonym *V. tomentosum*) is indigenous to China and Japan. **Characteristics:** This pretty flowering shrub is deciduous with widely outspread branches. The leaves are elliptical, up to 4″ long and dark green on top. The autumn coloration is dark red. The white blossoms appear in the form of a broad, flat cyme which turns pink when it withers. This shrub is hardy. **Growing Conditions:** For its optimal development, *V. plicatum* needs ordinary, nutrient-containing and water-retaining garden soil without puddles. It also tolerates light shade. **Varieties:** Although the single form blooms as early as May, the full bloom of the "Mariesii" variety first appears in June (illustration above). A very attractive variety is "Lanarth." Also worthy of mention are "Rowallane" and "Tomentosum"; the latter blooms in the form of a flat cyme about 4″ wide. Its fruits are initially red and then turn black. **Recommendations:** Because of its small size, *V. plicatum* can be used in many ways, either in combination with shrubs or summer flowers, as a solitary specimen, or in combination with other shrubs as part of a flowering border.

Viburnum carlesii   Fragrant Viburnum

Origin: Korea. **Characteristics:** This shrub has squarrose branches and forms an umbrella-shaped top. The deciduous leaves grow to a length of 2″–4″, are wide and ovate, slightly toothed, and grayish green. The small blossoms first appear a blush-pink, then turn white and stand in cymes 2″–3″ wide. They are distinguished by their intense and pleasant fragrance. **Growing Conditions:** *V. carlesii* likes sufficiently moist, nutrient-containing soil in protected spots a little away from the sun. **Species:** The following species are recommended: *V. x burkwoodii,* 6½'–10', evergreen, with oval to elliptical, shiny dark green leaves 1½″–2¾″ long; it blooms in April and May, at first red, then white in the form of fragrant corymbs. *V. x carlcephalum,* 6½' tall, white, globular blossoms in May, also fragrant. *V. lantana,* also called the Rugose Wayfaring Tree, 10'–16' tall, blooms in the form of white, flat cymes about 4″ wide; the poisonous fruit is initially red, then bluish black. *V. opulus,* 6½'–13' tall, plate-shaped blossoms in May and June; the shiny red berries are poisonous. *V. opulus* "Sterile" blooms in May with white ball-shaped cymes, probably the best-known variety. *V. rhytidophyllum* has evergreen leaves and grows to 6½'–13' in height. **Recommendations:** Since it is so modest in height, *V. carlesii* can stand alone in small gardens, rock gardens, or atrium gardens, or it can be planted in larger pots in combination with blooming shrubs or annuals.

Weigela hybrids

Height: 6½'–10'   Diameter: 5'–8'   Soil: 1   V–VI

Origin: The parent forms of our present *Weigela* hybrids are indigenous to Japan and China. The hybrids themselves have been cultivated through horticultural crossbreeding. **Characteristics:** The *Weigelas* rank among our most important flowering shrubs. Their full bloom occurs in May and June and immediately follows that of the lilac and the laburnum. In this way the *Weigela* hybrids form the transition, as it were, to the blooming seasons of the summer woody plants, primarily the roses. The *Weigela* hybrids are mostly distinguished by their vigorous growth and, on the other hand, are so restricted in their dimensions that they prove to be very versatile, particularly in private gardens. The dense, deciduous, partially overhanging boughs are distinguished by a profuse bloom, and the bell-shaped blossoms appear on the previous year's growth. The green leaves range from elliptical to elongated ovate and are pointed at the tip. **Growing Conditions:** The *Weigelas* like a sunny location with a medium heavy, sufficiently moist but well-drained soil rich in nutrients. Although they can tolerate a bit of shade, they develop much better in direct and full sunlight, especially as far as the profusion of blossoms is concerned. **Varieties and Species:** "Le Printemps," pink, early-blooming, hardy; "Fleur de Mai," pink, early-blooming, hardy; "Floreal," carmine red, early-blooming, resistant. Later, that is, in June, the following varieties come into bloom: "Abel Carriere," carmine pink; "Boskoop Glory," salmon pink; "Bristol Ruby," scarlet red; "Eva Supreme," dark red, more vigorous in growth than the previously mentioned variety; "Newport Red," dark red and likewise more vigorous than "Eva Rathke"; "Striaca," pink and rich in blossoms. In addition to the *Weigela* hybrids mentioned above, there are two more species that originate in the Far East and which deserve mention, even though they are far less available than the other hybrids. *W. florida* forms upright shrubs that grow to 10' with brownish-yellow branches distinguished by two clearly marked lines and covered with deciduous, elliptical leaves that can reach a length of 4". The pink blossoms appear in May and June and are somewhat lighter in the middle. The variety "Nana" grows into low shrubs with yellow-edged leaves and its blossoms are bright pink. "Purpurea" never grows taller than 10', is dense and bushy, and has red blossoms. The leaves are a reddish-green color. *W. middendorffiana* is a broad shrub that reaches a diameter of up to 13'. The deciduous leaves are long and oval and taper to a point. The blossoms (May and June) are sulfur-colored and have orange spots on the inside. **Recommendations:** Because of its limited size and its large number of varieties, the *Weigela* hybrids as well as other species of *Weigela* can be used for many purposes. They can be featured as solitary specimens on lawns or used in an arrangement of flowering shrubs as well as in roof gardens or in larger pots. Compatible partners for *Weigelas* are, among others, *Kolkwitzia, Lonicera morrowii,* and *Philadelphus.*

Aristolochia macrophylla   Dutchman's Pipe

Height: 33′   Soil: 1–3   V–VIII

Origin: *A. macrophylla* originates in the eastern part of the United States.
Characteristics: *A. macrophylla* is still known in some places under the synonyms *A. durior* and *A. sipho*. The Dutchman's Pipe is a twining vine that can easily reach a height of 33′ with the help of an appropriate support trellis. The expansive growth is dependent upon the understructure to be climbed. After *A. macrophylla* has reached the upper part of a pergola, for example, it can continue to grow several feet higher. Characteristic of this vine are its large (sometimes 12″ wide), heart-shaped dark green leaves that are arranged like shingles on a roof. The young shoots that give rise to these ornamental leaves are green. The blossoms of *A. macrophylla* appear mainly in May and June. Stragglers can appear as late as August. As a rule they sit under the leaves, are shaped like a Meerschaum pipe and look a little strange. These blossoms are yellowish green on the outside and brownish purple on the inside. In keeping with its origins, this twining vine is very hardy. Moreover, it is also pollution-resistant. **Growing Conditions:** Because of its vigorous growth and the large surface of the leaves, *A. macrophylla* needs a sufficiently moist, deep soil rich in clay and nutrients, but it should not have any standing water. Dutchman's Pipe can stand in direct sunlight as well as in partially shady or shady spots. **Recommendations:** This vine is excellently suited for covering walls, standing timbers, trestles, and pergolas. Since it can tolerate both sunny as well as shady locations, there is a considerable range of possible uses. It should be noted, however, that *A. macrophylla* always needs stakes or wire as supports.

Bilderdykia aubertii   Silver Fleece Vine

Height: 33'   Soil: 1–2   IX–X

Origin: *B. aubertii* is indigenous to Western China and Tibet and has become naturalized in various regions of Europe. The botanical nomenclature for this recommended twining vine is still undetermined. In addition to the name *Bilderdykia aubertii*, which is known in horticultural circles, there also exists the new scientific name *Fallopia aubertii* and the designation *Polygonum aubertii* commonly found in gardening catalogues. **Characteristics:** *B. aubertii* is distinguished by an enormous growth capacity which frequently makes a regular cutting back necessary. The deciduous leaves are oval and lance-shaped and taper to a point. The small, creamy white blossoms appear in the form of many rather large terminal panicles from August onward. **Growing Conditions:** The Silver Fleece Vine does not make any special claims concerning the soil. In good soil with a plentiful water supply it tends toward an opulent and luxuriant growth. It is therefore recommended to plant it whenever possible in poor soil with a none too ample supply of water. *B. aubertii* tolerates both sunny as well as partially shady spots. **Recommendations:** *B. aubertii* is exceptionally well suited for the rapid covering of unattractive walls, fences, and so forth. On flat surfaces it needs some support to climb on. As far as fences and comparable structures are concerned, all you need do is interweave this vine into a grounded trellis during the first years; it will soon take care of itself.

Celastrus orbiculatus   Oriental Bittersweet

Height: 33'–40'   Soil: 1–3   VI   E

Origin: *C. orbiculatus* is native to Japan, Manchuria, and China. Bittersweet has become naturalized in the eastern United States. **Characteristics:** Like *B. aubertii,* this is also a case of a rapidly growing twining vine. *C. orbiculatus* has a separate male and female plant and both are needed to obtain the desired yellow fruits, which, after they pop, expose shiny red seeds. The unpretentious yellowish-green blossoms appear in June in the form of cymes emanating from a central stem. **Growing Conditions:** None of the Bittersweets likes soil that is too dry, neither in full sunshine nor in partial shade. This twining vine is considered generally hardy. **Recommendations:** Oriental Bittersweet forms a good cover for large pergolas and walls. However, the support of a wire trellis is required. Bittersweet can also climb the trunks of old trees, but is not recommended for those of younger ones, for it is a strangler in the true sense of the word and prevents the tree from increasing in diameter.

Clematis x jackmanii   Jackman Clematis

Height: 10'   Diameter: 1½'   Soil: 1–5   ·   V–IX

Origin: *C. x jackmanii* was cultivated from a cross between *C. lanuginosa* and *C. viticella.* **Characteristics:** Among the ornamental clematis, *C. x jackmanii* (see illustration) is one of the hardiest and most vigorous varieties. The purplish-violet blossoms can reach a diameter of 4" and more. *C. x jackmanii* was used as one of the parent plants in the cultivation of the majority of *Clematis* hybrids. **Growing Conditions:** Like all clematis, *C. x jackmanii* demands a deep, nutrient-containing soil enriched at the time of planting and again in later years with ripe barnyard manure and carbonate of lime. The "foot" of the clematis must always be cool, which means covered. This can be assured by surrounding it with shade plants that consume few nutrients from the soil or by covering it with leaves. The above-ground parts can tolerate the sun. However, *C. x jackmanii* and the other varieties of clematis should not be planted on southern exposures, but rather in a location protected from the intense midday sun. The soil should always be sufficiently moist, but not as a result of a dripping gutter or similar source. **Varieties and Species:** The most popular of these plants are represented today by the *Clematis* hybrids, some of which will be described below. However, it must be remembered that the full bloom and its duration is highly dependent upon location. The following descriptions indicate the main blooming seasons. "Comtesse de Bouchard," silky, lavender, June to October. "Crimson King," wine red, July to September. "Edouard Desfosse," deep lilac, May to June. "Ernest Markham," red, hardy, July to September. "Henryi," large blossoms, white, July to August. "Huldine," white, medium-sized, very hardy, July to October. "Marcel Moser," very large blossoms, bluish white with reddish middle streaks, May to July. "Lasurstern," profuse pure deep blue blossoms with white filaments, May to June. "Lady Betty Balfour," deep purple, vigorous, September and October. "Marie Boisselot" (synonym "Mme Le Coultre"), pure white, June to August. "Mme Adouard André," profuse blossoms, amaranth red, July to September. "Nelly Moser," pale lilac, underside pure white, June and July. "Prins Hendrik," azure blue, very large blossoms, July to August. "The President," dark blue with a reddish underside, July and August. "Ville de Lyon," medium-sized blossoms, carmine red, July to September, sometimes sickly. Also noteworthy are the wild forms because they are distinguished by vigorous growth and hardiness. *C. montana* can climb up to 26' in height; it produces a large number of small white blossoms in spring followed in the fall by ornamental, silvery white featherlike fruits. *C. tangutica* reaches a height of about 10' and produces yellow bell-shaped blossoms in June which are followed in autumn by ornamental fruits. *C. vitalba* can also climb 26' high and is similar to *C. montana. C. viticella,* on the other hand, only grows to 6½', produces small violet blossoms in June and July and is particularly hardy. There are also white and pink blooming varieties. **Recommendations:** *C. x jackmanii,* like the other forms of clematis, is used as a green cover for pergolas, walls, garden terraces, doorways and fences, and in many cases needs a support structure.

Hedera helix   English Ivy

Height: 100′   Soil: 1–5   IX–X   ✳   E   !!!

Origin: *H. helix* has its natural habitat in Europe all the way to the Caucasus.
Characteristics: *H. helix* is a clinging vine which, with the help of its rootlike holdfasts, can climb to a height of 100′ on trees, walls, etc. The evergreen leaves have long stems and three to five lobes in the early stages of growth. They are about 4″ long and have brightly marked veins. Somewhat smaller, ovate-rhombic, smooth-edged leaves form on the flowering shoots of older plants. Blossoms first appear on older plants. Typical in this respect are the old ivy plants on the walls of castles and other ancient buildings. The globose flowers appear only late in the year (September and October until the onset of winter), and the black, somewhat globular fruit only in the following year. The berries, like the other parts of this plant, are poisonous, but they are so bitter to the taste that children hardly ever touch them. **Growing Conditions:** *H. helix* prefers deep, alkaline soil with an ample supply of water with no puddles. The location should be partially shady to shady. Nevertheless, if accustomed to it from the very beginning, this clinging vine can also tolerate sunny locations. **Varieties and Species:** "Conglomerata," dwarf ivy, bushy shoots with dense, tortuously intertwined grayish-green leaves; especially suited for regions with mild winters. "Erecta," similar to "Minima," dwarf ivy, with a dense growth of leaves, each with three to five lobes, also suited for places with deep shade. "Sagittaefolia" with leaves shaped like arrowheads, very graceful variety. "Argenteovariegata," variegated leaves. "Aureovariegata," yellowish leaves. *H. colchica* is indigenous to the Caucasus and northern Anatolia and is especially suited as a ground cover. *H. colchica* "Arborescens" grows in broad shrub form and reaches up to 3′ in height; the greenish-yellow blossoms appear in September, followed by black berries. *H. colchica* "Dentata" has heavily denticulated leaves, and "Dentatovariegata" has, in addition, a white stripe along the edge of the leaf. *H. hibernica* (frequently identified in catalogues as the species "Hibernica") is native to Ireland and is distinguished by a more vigorous growth than *H. helix* and by larger leaves. *H. hibernica* is supposed to be less frost-resistant and generally does not bloom and bear fruit. The veins of the leaves are clearly and brightly marked and the middle lobe is accentuated. **Recommendations:** *H. helix* is frequently used nowadays as a ground cover in shady spots under trees. Moreover, this clinging vine is well suited for covering walls or for climbing on trellises, large tree trunks, etc. The less vigorously growing varieties of *H. helix* described above can be used in many ways within the limits of a private garden. This versatility is also due in part to the fact that ivy is hardy and pollution-resistant.

Hydrangea anomala ssp. petiolaris Climbing Hydrangea

Height: 33'   Soil: 1   VI–VIII

Origin: *H. anomala ssp. petiolaris* is indigenous to Japan and has become naturalized in Korea and Formosa. **Characteristics:** In keeping with its growth characteristics, this vine is also known as Climbing Hydrangea among experts and flower lovers. The bald reddish-brown shoots, like the ivy, can climb a wall to a height of 33' with the help of their rootlike holdfasts. The deciduous leaves have an elongated heart shape and taper to a point. They grow to between 2″ and 4″ long. The blossoms appear on the previous year's short shoots. They form flat corymbs that can attain a diameter of up to almost 8″. The external sterile blossoms and the internal fertile blossoms are creamy white. Moreover, the sterile blossoms are larger than the fertile ones. The tiny white "petals" of the blossoms are not petals at all, but rather bracteoles, which replace the blossom petals. *H. anomala ssp. petiolaris* is prettiest during its full bloom from June to August and in the fall as a result of its golden yellow coloration. This clinging vine is considered hardy and pollution-resistant. **Growing Conditions:** Climbing Hydrangeas do not make any particular demands on their location. They can flourish in sunny as well as in partially shady or shady spots. The soil should be sufficiently deep and moist, but free from standing water. **Recommendations:** *H. anomala ssp. petiolaris* is well suited for covering both house and garden walls and can also be employed as a climbing cover for pergolas and trellises. Because of its ability to tolerate shade, this species can also be planted on northern exposures.

Lonicera x tellmanniana   Tellman Honeysuckle

Origin: *L. x tellmanniana* was developed by crossing *L. sempervirens* with *L. tragophylla*. **Characteristics:** This honeysuckle is a large twining vine with deep green deciduous leaves 2"–4" in length and elliptical in shape. They grow onto the ends of the shoots in a plate-shaped arrangement. The tubular, shiny, yellowish-orange fragrant blossoms appear from May to July in dense whorls on the ends of the shoots. These are followed by highly ornamental coral red berries. On the whole, *L. x tellmanniana* is a hardy plant well suited for an urban environment. **Growing Conditions:** Tellman Honeysuckle loves a sunny location above all else, but it can also tolerate some shade. There are no special soil requirements, but for vigorous growth the soil should be sufficiently moist. **Species:** *L. caprifolium*, known as Sweet Honeysuckle, has become naturalized from Central Europe to Asia Minor. This species grows to about 13'. It is deciduous and produces a profusion of tubular yellowish-white blossoms that are faintly pink on the outside. The blossoms are about 1½"–2" in length and appear in May and June; they are followed by coral red berrylike fruits. **Recommendations:** Like the other clinging species of *Lonicera*, *L. x tellmanniana*, too, is highly appropriate for pergolas, or for covering old walls, fences, and so on. On flat surfaces this twining vine needs some structural support.

Lonicera x heckrottii   Everblooming Honeysuckle

Origin: *L. x heckrottii* was cultivated from a cross between *L. x americana* and *L. sempervirens*. **Characteristics:** *L. x heckrottii* is a vigorous vinelike plant with deciduous, long dark green oval leaves that do not grow together. The tubular blossoms are yellow inside and faintly pink on the outside, and they give off a strong fragrance. The carmine red berries appear later in dense clusters. **Growing Conditions:** *L. x heckrottii* does not make any special claims except that it be located in a sunny spot with sufficiently moist soil. **Species:** *L. x brownii* was bred by crossing *L. hirsuta* with *L. sempervirens*. This twining vine grows to a height of 10'–13'. Especially ornamental is the variety *L. x brownii* "Dropmore Scarlet," which produces tubular blossoms in terminal tufts which range in color from blood orange to deep red. The location should be sunny. *L. henryi* is indigenous to China, grows to 10'–13' high and has very hairy shoots. The shiny dark green evergreen leaves are long and lance-shaped and ciliated on the edge. The yellowish-red tubular blossoms appear from June to August and are about ¾" long. **Recommendations:** Essentially the same as *L. x tellmanniana*. Experts consider *L. x heckrottii* the most beautiful species of clinging honeysuckle.

Parthenocissus tricuspidata   Boston Ivy

Origin: Japan, Korea, and China. **Characteristics:** *P. tricuspidata* is a clinging vine with enormous growth potential. Typical is the seemingly slow growth in the beginning which increases in geometric progression after an initial period of two to three years and which can lead to the climbing and covering of surfaces measuring many square yards. This is possible because *P. tricuspidata* has short climbing shoots that end in suckerlike holdfasts. The leaves are deciduous and are composed of three-pointed lobes coarsely denticulated. The reddish growth and the reddish-orange to scarlet autumn coloring are glorious. Blossom and fruit are insignificant. **Growing Conditions:** *P. tricuspidata* tolerates both direct sunlight as well as shady locations. It does not make any particular requirements of the soil, but thrives well in a deep, moist soil rich in nutrients and free from standing water. **Variety:** As a rule, "Veitchii" is the most available variety and it is distinguished by a particularly beautiful leaf coloration. **Recommendations:** Considered hardy and pollution-resistant, *P. tricuspidata* is exceptionally well suited for covering walls of any kind; a freeze-back is possible in severe winter weather. In contrast to older plants, young specimens of *P. tricuspidata* frequently fare poorly and produce only thin shoots. When planting, one should cut these shoots back about halfway so that they branch out and climb along the surface in a fan-shaped direction.

Parthenocissus quinquefolia   Virginia Creeper

Origin: Central and Eastern North America. **Characteristics:** With the help of an appropriate support structure, this vine uses its climbing tendrils to scale considerable heights. The deciduous long-stemmed leaves have five sections. Each individual leaflet is elliptical, usually somewhat denticulated and a dull green in color during the vegetation period. The reddish shoots and particularly the shiny red to carmine red autumn coloration are strikingly ornamental. Blossoms and fruit are lacking in any special significance, and small black berrylike fruits are produced. **Growing Conditions:** These correspond to those of *P. tricuspidata.* **Variety:** "Engelmannii" differs from the species described above in its graceful shape, its more intensive autumn coloration, and in the fact that the climbing tendrils have holdfasts. **Recommendations:** The Virginia Creeper is a very good climbing cover for pergolas, old tree trunks and, in particular instances, for climbing over high hedges. It has proven to be hardy and pollution-resistant, but it can freeze-back during extremely severe winters. Because of its holdfasts, "Engelmannii" can also be used to cover large flat walls, just like *P. tricuspidata.* In contrast to the latter, however, one should not use *P. quinquefolia* "Engelmannii" on northern exposures.

Wisteria sinensis   Chinese Wisteria

Height: 33′   Soil: 1   V–VI   !!!

Origin: As its name already indicates, *W. sinensis* is indigenous to China.
Characteristics: *Wisteria* is a vigorously growing twining vine which needs an appropriate support structure. The young gray shoots have no trouble in attaining a height of 33′ if the plant has the optimal supply of nutrients, water, and support from the necessary trellis. The deciduous leaves are composed of from 10 to 13 lance-shaped compound leaves. The individual pinna leaflet is pointed and ranges between 1½″ and 3″ long. The leaves of the Wisteria tend to fade somewhat after blooming. Careful dosages of nitrogen and iron-rich fertilizer act against this. The papilionaceous flowers are bright bluish violet and grow to about 1″ in width. They appear in May or June depending upon their location, have a delicate fragrance, and are arranged in a dense row of clusters that can extend to up to 10″ in length. Well-selected specimens distinguish themselves by an enormous profusion of blossoms. **Growing Conditions:** *Wisteria* likes warm, protected locations and finds a region conducive to the growing of grapes ideal. In more rugged locations you should provide a winter protection by draping the upper portions with brushwood from fir trees and by packing the lower portions with hay. In this way the trunk and the shoots are protected from the winter sun and are not so mercilessly exposed to drying winds. The soil should be deep, rich in nutrients, and well supplied with water. This is particularly necessary during the blooming season, when the moisture needs of this twining vine, like that of other profusely blooming plants, are particularly great. **Species and Varieties:** *W. floribunda* is indigenous to Japan and has become naturalized in several parts of the United States. It blooms in the period from May to July in the form of long clusters of violet papilionaceous blossoms. Unlike *W. sinensis,* this species is distinguished by a less vigorous growth, for it generally does not grow taller than 16′. This is a particular advantage for smaller gardens. *W. floribunda* ''Alba'' has white blossoms; ''Issai'' is considered especially pretty and produces an abundance of bright blue blossoms. ''Macrobotrys'' has long, loosely constructed blossom clusters with bluish-violet individual flowers; the blossom clusters of this variety can reach far beyond 20″ in length. *W. floribunda* ''Rosea'' blooms a bright lavender color.
Recommendations: Under the growing conditions described above, *Wisteria* is exceptionally well suited for covering walls if it is given an appropriate support structure. In the beginning it is a good idea to guide the young shoots by tying them in such a way that the vine is evenly distributed over the surface of the wall. *Wisteria* makes an excellent climbing arrangement for pergolas or other similar structures. Since it blooms at approximately the same time as the laburnum, these two plants can be situated close to each other to make the most of their contrasting colors. Like the other species of *Wisteria, W. sinensis* is poisonous, and this is why it should not be planted where children play or in places that are accessible to small children without adult supervision.

Index

Common English names of plants are listed first; botanical designations follow.

Look for these other books in the Macmillan Gardening series

THE MACMILLAN BOOK OF NATURAL HERB GARDENING
by Marie-Luise Kreuter

THE MACMILLAN BOOK OF ORGANIC GARDENING
by Marie-Luise Kreuter

Look for these other gardening books from Macmillan

WYMAN'S GARDENING ENCYCLOPEDIA
by Donald Wyman

THE TREASURY OF HOUSEPLANTS
by Rob Herwig and Margot Schubert

THE MACMILLAN TREASURY OF HERBS
by Ann Bonar